P9-DVA-939

12 MONTHS OF FUN!

THE LOBSTER KIDS' GUIDE
TO EXPLORING
SAN FRANCISCO

BY DAVID COLE
AND MARY LEE TREES COLE

Lobster Press™

Cole, David, 1945-
Trees Cole, Mary Lee, 1941-
The Lobster Kids' Guide to Exploring San Francisco: 12 Months of Fun!
Text copyright © 2001 by Lobster Press™
Illustrations copyright © 2001 by Lobster Press™

All rights reserved. No part of this publication may be reproduced, stored in any retrieval system or transmitted, in any form or by any means, without the prior written permission of Lobster Press™.

Published by
Lobster Press™
1620 Sherbrooke St. W., Suites C & D
Montréal, Québec H3H 1C9
Tel. (514) 904-1100, Fax (514) 904-1101
www.lobsterpress.com

Publisher: Alison Fripp
Editor: Bob Kirner
Assistant Editor: Alison Fischer
Copy Editor: Frances Purslow
Cover and Illustrations: Christine Battuz
Icons: Christiane Beauregard and Josée Masse
Layout and Design: Olivier Lasser

Distribution:
In the United States   In Canada
Advanced Global Distribution Services   Raincoast Books
5880 Oberlin Drive, Suite 400   9050 Shaughnessey Street
San Diego, CA 92121   Vancouver, BC V6P 6E5
Tel. (858) 457-2500   Tel. 1-800-663-5714
Fax (858) 812-6476   Fax 1-800-565-3770

We acknowledge the financial support of the Government of Canada through the Book Publishing Industry Development Program (BPIDP) for our publishing activities.

National Library of Canada Cataloguing in Publication Data

Cole, David, 1945-
The Lobster kids' guide to exploring San Francisco: 12 months of fun!

Includes Index.
ISBN 1-894222-28-8

    1. Family recreation—California—San Francisco—
Guidebooks. 2. Children—Travel—California—San Francisco—
Guidebooks. 3. Amusements—California—San Francisco—
Guidebooks. 4. San Francisco (Calif.)—Guidebooks. I. Cole,
Mary Lee Trees, 1941– II. Battuz, Christine III. Kirner, Bob,
1959– IV. Title

F869.S33C64 2001   917.94'610454   C2001-900033-2

Printed and bound in Canada

Table of Contents

Authors' Introduction

Our family has lived in the Bay Area for many years, however we are continually discovering new and wonderful things to enjoy. San Francisco is a huge tourist destination, offering world-class museums, green spaces, historical sites and theater—places where families can play and learn together. But there are plenty of neighborhood attractions too, such as libraries, bowling alleys and community centers, where you won't have to line up to visit.

In the process of writing this book, we have had the opportunity to return to many of our favorite haunts and to visit new places we have always wanted to see. As our list of "must-see" destinations began to grow so did our appreciation for the region we call home. We couldn't include all the things for families in the Bay Area. It would take many more pages than there are in this guide. Instead, we have focused on the best things for families in San Francisco, as well as some fabulous attractions in East Bay, Marin and the Peninsula. We hope you have as many fun-filled and memorable hours discovering this amazing family-friendly area as we did re-discovering it.

We want to acknowledge our son, Aaron, who helped us explore many destinations that we would never have found on our own. Our thanks go to our editor, Bob Kirner, our publisher, Alison Fripp, and all our friends who shared information and enthusiastic reports on where to go next.

DAVID COLE AND MARY LEE TREES COLE

A Word from the Publisher

Lobster Press™ published its first book, *The Lobster Kids' Guide to Exploring Montréal* in 1998. Since then, the Kids' City Explorers Series has grown and now includes guides to other major Canadian cities. Due to the resounding success of the Canadian series, this year Lobster Press™ is publishing books for families exploring cities in the United States.

Whether you're a tourist, resident, parent or teacher, this book is a complete resource of things to do and see with kids in the San Francisco area. It's jam-packed with valuable, timesaving information and great ideas for outings.

David Cole, Mary Lee Trees Cole and their son visited the sites in this guide in 2000-2001. All information provided has been verified. However, since prices and business hours are subject to change, call ahead to avoid disappointment. Please accept our apologies in advance for any inconveniences you may encounter.

To get the most out of this guide, please familiarize yourself with our "Lobster Rating System" and table of icons. These features let you know what our authors' family thought of each site and what amenities are available.

If you have comments about this book, visit our website and complete our on-line survey. Let us know if we've missed your family's favorite destination, and we'll include it in the next edition!

One last word: Please be careful when you and your children visit the sites from the guide. Neither

Lobster Press™ nor the authors can be held responsible for any accidents that might occur.

Enjoy! And watch for the other books in the Kids' City Explorers Series. Now available: Boston, Chicago, Seattle and Las Vegas. Coming in 2002: Halifax, Miami, New Orleans, Québec City and San Diego.

FROM THE GANG AT LOBSTER PRESS™

The Lobster Rating System

We thought it would be helpful if you knew what the Cole family thought about the sites in this book before you head off to visit them. They rated every attraction and activity they visited for its:

☞ enjoyment level for children
☞ learning opportunities for children
☞ accessibility from downtown
☞ costs and value for the money

A one-lobster rating: Good attraction.

A two-lobster rating: Very good attraction.

A three-lobster rating: Excellent attraction.

Not fitting some of the criteria, and subsequently not rated, are green spaces and various similar, nearby or other attractions.

Table of Icons

These facilities and/or activities are represented by the following icons:

Bart station		Picnic tables	
Beach		Playground	
Bicycling		Restaurant/ snack bar	
Birthday parties			
Bus stop		Restroom	
First aid		Skating	
Hiking		Swimming	
In-line skating		Telephone	
Information centre		Trolley/Cable car stop	
Parking		Wheelchair/stroller accessible	
		Wildlife watching	

CHAPTER 1

LOCAL
ATTRACTIONS

Introduction

San Francisco is the most popular tourist destination in the U.S. and one of the most desirable places to live—and for good reason. As any resident or visitor will tell you, there is an endless variety of interesting things to do and places to see, situated in a magnificent natural setting. The mild year-round weather allows kids to enjoy these sites anytime. San Francisco is set on a peninsula between the Pacific Ocean and a bay, ringed with mountains and coastal hills containing miles of parks, forests and ecology preserves. The metropolitan area is home to 6.5 million people, with hundreds of neighborhoods and local parks, museums, entertainment centers, historical sites, sports and recreation facilities. With all this incredible variety, there are a few must-see favorites—many are free or inexpensive. A walk on Golden Gate Bridge, boating in Golden Gate Park, riding cable cars up and down steep hills, strolling through Chinatown, checking out street artists at Ghirardelli or Union Square, or playing in the gardens at Zeum—these are favorites of visitors from all over the world that locals need not wait for out-of-town guests to enjoy.

Check Out "The Rock"
ALCATRAZ

San Francisco Bay, San Francisco
(415) 705-5555
www.nps.gov/Alcatraz

Alcatraz, Spanish for pelican, was named for the birds that were the island's original inhabitants. A military fort in the 1850s, the island went on to become a prison. First for Spanish-American War prisoners and then in 1934 for some of the country's most notorious criminals. Al Capone, George "Machine Gun" Kelly and Robert "Birdman of Alcatraz" Stroud lived here.

Only a mile from shore, no prisoner ever escaped across the icy bay from this maximum-security stronghold. At the time, it was the only federal prison with hot showers—a luxury to keep inmates from becoming acclimatized to cold water. A federal penitentiary until 1963, "The Rock" is now a popular tourist attraction. The 12-acre island is accessible only by ferry that departs from Fisherman's Wharf. A visit to Alcatraz is as good as its hype. After the short, scenic ferry ride to the infamous island, take your own self-guided tour. See the eerie cell block, mess hall and dark solitary confinement chambers. A top-notch audio tour narrated by former inmates and prison guards is available for an additional fee.

SEASONS AND TIMES

➤ Year-round: Daily, 9:30 am—2:15 pm. Reservations suggested. Call the above number, or (415) 773-1188.

COST

➤ Individuals (12 and up) $12, seniors (62 and up) $10.50, children (5 to 11) $7.

GETTING THERE

➤ By car, from Market St., drive northeast until the San Francisco Ferry Building. Turn north on The Embarcadero and continue on to Fisherman's Wharf and the Pier 39 parking structure. You may find street parking within several blocks of Pier 41. About 10 minutes from the Ferry building.

➤ By public transit, take Muni Metro (F line).

NEARBY

➤ Pier 39, Fisherman's Wharf, USS *Pampanito*, SS *Jeremiah O'Brien*, Wax Museum, Ripley's Believe It or Not.

COMMENT

➤ Wear comfortable shoes and dress warmly, whatever the season. Children in strollers should be tucked into a warm blanket. Plan a 3- to 4-hour visit.

Take a Quick Trip to
CHINATOWN

**Gateway Arch (corner of Bush St. and Grant Ave.),
San Francisco
www.sfchinatown.com**

E ven on foggy days Chinatown teems with interesting sights—residents ranging from children to great-grandparents, stores full of unusual food and delicious aromas, shops with amazing trinkets and quality imported goods and restaurants serving up tasty dishes.

Start your visit at the Gateway Arch on the corner of Bush Street and Grant Avenue. Passing through the gate you enter Chinatown, home of one of the largest Chinese populations outside of Asia. Don't miss the Bank of America and the other buildings with traditional Chinese architectural style. Ask your kids how many dragons they can find. The Chinatown Kite Shop (717 Grant Street) offers an incredible assortment of flying objects for the beach or park. Feeling peckish? There is no end to the shops where your family can enjoy a quick dim sum snack of dumplings and sweet buns. If you have time, proceed up Jackson Street to Ross Alley and walk by the Golden Gate Fortune Cookie Company. Its doors are often open so you can peek inside. One block west of Grant Street is Waverly Place (The Street of Painted Balconies), a Chinese version of a New Orleans street. Bring your cameras and camcorders!

Events are going on continually in Chinatown and many, like Chinese New Year (page 219), are suitable for families. For a rundown of current happenings, visit the website given above.

SEASONS AND TIMES
→ Year-round: Daily. It's best to visit during daylight hours when shops are open.

COST
→ Free.

GETTING THERE
→ By car, from U.S. 80, take the Fremont Exit to downtown and follow the signs to Chinatown. Park in the Sutter-Stockton, St. Mary's Square or Portsmouth Square garages. About 15 minutes from U.S. 80.

➤ By public transit, take Muni buses 1, 12 or 15. Or take the cable car that runs along California St.

NEARBY
➤ Portsmouth Square (a plaza and meeting place with a colorful play structure), Chinese Cultural Center (third floor of the Holiday Inn at 750 Kearny), Chinese Historical Society of America Museum (Commercial St. near Kearny).

COMMENT
➤ Wear comfortable walking shoes. Plan a 1- to 4-hour visit.

Colorful, Entertaining
FISHERMAN'S WHARF
AND GHIRARDELLI
SQUARE

Jefferson St. between Larkin and Powell streets,
San Francisco
(415) 775-5500 (Ghirardelli Square)
www.ghirardellisq.com
www.fishermanswharf.org

Everyone needs to visit Fisherman's Wharf at least once. A good place to begin is Ghirardelli Square, west of the wharf on Jefferson Street. The Square, once a historic factory converted into a retail complex, offers 10 floors with 50 shops, cafés, restaurants and places to admire the spectacular view. Free entertainment abounds; street performers regularly put on shows. Don't miss the Ghirardelli Chocolate Manufactory and Soda Fountain at the

Polka Street entrance. You can watch chocolate being made while enjoying gooey ice cream treats. Near the Square is the cable car turnaround where you can hop on a cable car ($2 a ride) for an exciting journey up San Francisco's hills. At Christmas time, festive decorations in the Square are lit with millions of tiny lights.

To check out Fisherman's Wharf, wander down Jefferson Street with its lively street scenes of artists, mimes and musicians. You will pass The Cannery (415-771-3112; www.thecannery.com), a fruit-canning factory transformed into charming shops. Pause for a snack and take in the entertainment. Amid the fresh seafood stands and souvenir shops look for Richard Henry Dana Street, often referred to as "Fish Alley," where you will see what remains of the huge fishing fleet. Come early if you want to view fishermen bringing in their day's catch. Jefferson Street also houses Ripley's "Believe It Or Not!" Museum (415-771-6188; www.ripleysf.com) and the newly renovated Wax Museum Entertainment Complex (1-800-439-4305; www.waxmuseum.com) with hundreds of meticulously hand-created wax replicas of famous people.

SEASONS AND TIMES
→ Fisherman's Wharf and Ghirardelli Square: Year-round, daily. Businesses keep their own hours. Call the numbers above or visit the websites for specific dates and times.

COST
→ Free to wander and browse. Establishments, including Ripley's and the wax museum, charge admission.

GETTING THERE

➤ By car, from The Embarcadero, take North Point St. west to any of the streets beyond Powell St. Look for parking on the street or in public pay lots. The on-site pay parking is expensive. About 10 minutes from The Embarcadero.

➤ By public transit, take Muni buses 30, 32 or 42. Or take the Muni Metro (F line) to Fisherman's Wharf. The Powell-Mason and Powell-Hyde cable cars do their turnarounds at the wharf.

NEARBY

➤ Hyde Street Pier, Maritime National Historical Park, Aquatic Park, USS *Pampanito*, Blue & Gold Fleet for Bay sightseeing and trips to Alcatraz, Pier 39.

COMMENT

➤ Carry jackets in your daypacks since it is usually breezy. Plan a 2- to 6- hour visit.

Walk on the World Famous
GOLDEN GATE BRIDGE

The Golden Gate of San Francisco
www.goldengate.org

Walk onto the Golden Gate Bridge—the famous entrance to San Francisco. Let your kids experience the thrill of the sweeping views—from the Bay's hills and islands, including Alcatraz (page 15), to the Pacific Ocean. Two hundred feet beneath you pass tankers, tugboats, cruise ships and racing sailboats. Daring windsurfers dart in and out of the waves while foghorns and buoys sound their lonely warning. Your family can spend an hour or an entire day on a bridge excursion. If weather permits, you may want to pack a lunch and walk the three-mile round trip.

Start at the visitor plaza on the San Francisco side where bathrooms, snack bars, souvenir shops and information about the bridge are found. Check out the statue of Joseph B. Straus, the engineer who overcame incredible obstacles and dire predictions that "it couldn't be done." Nearby, you can touch a cross-section of the bridge's massive main cable and learn fascinating facts about the structure. For example, did you know that stretched end to end the bridge's cables could encircle the equator more than three times? Or that the concrete in the piers and anchorages could pave a five-foot-wide sidewalk from New York to San Francisco? Or that the roadway sways up to 27 feet to withstand winds of 100 miles per hour?

On weekdays and Saturdays, walkers are routed onto the bridge's east walkway and bicyclists use the one on the west. The directions are reversed on Sundays and holidays. Safety rails and fencing keep pedestrians (especially free-ranging tots) and cyclists away from the edge of the bridge and protect them from traffic.

SEASONS AND TIMES
➤ Pedestrian access: Year-round, daily, 5 am—9 pm.

COST
➤ Free.

GETTING THERE
➤ By car, take Rte. 1 N. from Golden Gate Park or U.S. 101 N. from Marina Blvd. and follow the signs to the visitor plaza. There is metered parking. About 10 minutes from Golden Gate Park.
➤ By public transit, Muni bus 29 stops at the visitor plaza.

NEARBY
➤ Fort Point, Golden Gate National Recreation Area, Sausalito.

COMMENT
➤ Wear flat walking shoes and dress warmly, whatever the season. Children in strollers should be tucked into a warm blanket. Avoid visiting during heavy commute hours if possible. Plan a 1- to 4-hour visit.

Tons of Fun
GOLDEN GATE PARK

Bordered by The Great Highway, Fulton St., Stanyan St. and Lincoln Way, San Francisco
(415) 391-2000
www.ci.sf.ca.us/info.htm

Picture an enormous 1,000-acre backyard with activities galore. That is Golden Gate Park. Once just sand dunes, the largest man-made park in the world now offers boating, hiking, racing model boats, picnicking, riding horses, interesting attractions and so much more.

On Sundays, John F. Kennedy Drive (the park's main roadway) is closed to car traffic allowing families to bike, skate and walk its length. Skate and bike rentals are available along Stanyan Street. Or, visit the Buffalo Paddock, where kids get a close-up look at these huge creatures, famous in American folklore and history. The Children's Playground has new play structures with cool slides. Nearby, the 1914 Herschell-Spillman Carousel sports 62 beautiful, hand-carved animals. Children eight and older can take horseback-riding lessons at the Equestrian Center. Or steer the gang to the Strybing Arboretum's Garden of Fragrance to test their sense of smell, touch and taste.

The Japanese Tea Garden and Teahouse has a charming garden with an undulating dragon hedge that leads to the "wishing bridge." Kids can climb the steep arch, make a wish, and throw a coin into the pond. Waitresses in traditional Japanese kimonos serve tea and cookies at the teahouse.

For a truly delightful time, head to Strawberry Hill and Stow Lake and rent a boat (cushion-style life preservers are supplied). Tell your kids to watch for ducks, turtles and swans. Across the bridge on the island, there is a peace pagoda and a waterfall that demand exploration. Stairs and paths lead up to a pretty picnic spot on Strawberry Hill. Though beware of seagulls that carry off sandwiches.

The M.H. de Young Memorial Museum (page 111) and the California Academy of Sciences (page 88) are also found in Golden Gate Park.

SEASONS AND TIMES
➤ Park: Year-round, daily. Attractions in the park have their own schedules. McClaren Lodge and Park Headquarters (415-831-2700) is open weekdays and has park information.

COST
➤ Park admission is free. There are fees for the Carousel, boat rentals, Japanese Tea Garden and horseback riding.

GETTING THERE

➤ By car, from U.S. 101, take Fell St. west to the park entrance on John F. Kennedy Dr. Free parking on site. About 20 minutes from U.S. 101.

➤ By public transit, Muni buses 5, 6, 7, 16AX, BX, 28, 29, 44, 66 and 71 all stop here. Or take the Muni Metro (N-Judah line).

NEARBY

➤ Steinhart Aquarium, Morrison Planetarium, Asian Art Museum.

COMMENT

➤ Wear comfortable walking shoes, dress in layers and put on sunscreen. Bring water bottles, snacks or lunches in backpacks. A ball, kite, or other favorite outdoor games add to the fun. Plan on anywhere from 1 to 6 hours.

Check Out What's Happening at
PIER 39

Beach St. and The Embarcadero, San Francisco
(415) 981-PIER (7437)
www.pier39.com

L ocated at the eastern end of Fisherman's Wharf, Pier 39 was originally a cargo pier. Today, the four-and-a-half acre site is a multilevel complex with more than 100 specialty shops in a recreated old-fashioned street scene. Here, you can buy everything from toys to candy and unique mementos. There are restaurants as well as fast-food stands and entertainment for all ages.

Younger kids enjoy the two-tiered Venetian carousel and NamcoLand, a large arcade. Pre-teens and teens will gravitate to Cyberstation to play video games, bumper cars and games of skill. Turbo Ride has four different motion-simulated adventures that will appeal to everyone. Don't forget to check out the magicians, jugglers, clowns and other artists who perform to delighted crowds on the Center Stage. For an exciting look at the city's colorful past and present history, see *The Great San Francisco Adventure* at the big-screen Cinemax Theater.

Underwater World, the pier's latest major addition, is a 707,000-gallon habitat in the Bay complete with sharks, salmon, stingrays and other West Coast marine life. A moving footpath hundreds of feet long takes you through clear acrylic tunnels inside the habitat while outside, the sea life swims all around. One of Pier 39's most popular attractions is free and features an endlessly entertaining colony of sea lions that bark, frolic and sleep on the nearby docks.

SEASONS AND TIMES
➤ Year-round: Daily, 10:30 am—8:30 pm. Extended summer hours. Most full-service restaurants open at 11:30 am.

COST
➤ Free to wander and browse. There are fees for special attractions. Call the number above or visit the website for details.

GETTING THERE
➤ By car, from downtown, take The Embarcadero north to Pier 39. Parking is available at the Pier 39 lot or on adjacent streets. About 15 minutes from downtown.

➤ By public transit, take Muni buses 30, 32 or 42. Or take the Muni Metro (F line) to Fisherman's Wharf.

NEARBY
➤ USS *Pampanito*, Blue & Gold Fleet for Bay sightseeing and trips to Alcatraz, Frequent Flyers bungee trampoline attraction, SS *Jeremiah O'Brien*.

COMMENT
➤ Pier 39 regularly sponsors special festivals and events that appeal to kids. Plan a 2- to 5-hour visit.

The Heart of San Francisco
UNION SQUARE

Bordered by Powell, Geary, Stockton and Post streets, San Francisco

San Francisco's primo shopping district and people-watching area is Union Square. It is decked with flower stalls, arts and craft stands, mimes (this is where Robin Williams got his start), musicians, pigeons and an amazing parade of people from all over the world. Packed into the surrounding streets are outstanding hotels and elegant shops. Among them is the not-to-be-missed FAO Schwarz Fifth Avenue toy store for children of all ages. If your kids are movie fans, they'll find fascinating mementos from their favorite films at Planet Hollywood. The Virgin Megastore, created for the musically inclined, is near the Square and so is a Border's super bookstore with a café. For young athletes, Niketown is a must.

Maiden Lane, a charming pedestrian street off Union Square, abounds with outdoor cafés. Choose a table streetside and take in the entertaining street musicians. A striking brick building designed by Frank Lloyd Wright as a prototype for New York's Guggenheim Museum resides on Maiden Lane. Go inside and look around. San Francisco's theater district is a step away from the West Side of the Square. On the East Side, a ticket booth sells same-day theater tickets at half-price. San Francisco's famous cable cars ($2 a ride) run on the Powell Street side of the Square. Hop on board one from any corner and ride over Nob Hill to Fisherman's Wharf (page 18).

During the Christmas season, Union Square is the center of the city's festivities with a tree lighting ceremony, carolers and beautifully decorated stores.

SEASONS AND TIMES
➤ Stores (generally): Year-round, Mon—Sat, 10 am—6 pm; Sun, noon—5 pm.

COST
➤ Exploring the square is free.

GETTING THERE
➤ By car, from The Embarcadero, take Geary Ave. west to Union Square and park at Union Square Garage (located under the square), or at one of the many nearby parking structures. Minutes from The Embarcadero.
➤ By public transit, take any of the Market St. buses. They all run near Union Square as do the Powell-Hyde and Powell-Mason cable car lines. Or take BART or the Muni Metro to the Powell Street station.

NEARBY
➤ San Francisco Centre.

COMMENT
➤ For a special treat, visit The Cheesecake Factory on the 8th floor of Macy's in Union Square (415-391-4444), where you can sample one of the 200 varieties of cheesecake and enjoy the view. Plan a 2- to 4-hour visit.

The Family-friendly Big U
UNIVERSITY OF CALIFORNIA AT BERKELEY

**Visitor Information Center, 101 University Hall, 220 University Ave., Berkeley
(510) 642-5215
www.berkeley.edu.**

Bring the kids and a ball to toss when you visit the University of California at Berkeley. Known for its academic excellence and distinguished faculty, the university boasts a scenic 1,200-acre campus with creeks and meadows. It's a great spot for a family outing. Free tours are offered, or use the self-guided tour map (available at the Visitor Information Center) and find these interesting places with your junior navigators leading the way. The Botanical Garden in lush Strawberry Canyon is a "library of living plants," covering more than 34 acres. Stop at the greenhouse and see the carnivorous plant exhibits and lily pond with colorful koi. The canyon has hiking trails and houses the popular Strawberry Recreation Facility with its swimming and wading pools.

The 30-story-tall Sather Tower, known simply as "The Campanile," is the centerpiece of the campus. You can ride the elevator 200 feet up to an observation platform and pick out familiar landmarks. When classes are in session, the tower's 61-bell carillon plays a noontime concert. Elsewhere on the campus, the Phoebe Hearst Museum of Anthropology has fascinating exhibits that showcase its more than four million artifacts, including amazing masks, tools and hunting spears. You can check out some very cool fossils at the Museum of Paleontology—among them the skeletons of a saber tooth tiger and a *Tyrannosaurus Rex*. The University Art Museum has an outdoor sculpture garden that kids love exploring. Inside, the café serves yummy snacks. The nearby Pacific Film Archive offers a variety of children's programs.

SEASONS AND TIMES
➛ Campus: Year-round, daily. The museums' schedules vary. Call the number given above for specific dates and times, visit the website or contact the Information Desk in the Martin Luther King, Jr. Student Union at Telegraph and Bancroft avenues.

COST
➛ Exploring the campus is free. Sather Tower and Botanical Garden (510-642-3343), the Phoebe Hearst Museum (510-642-3682), Strawberry Canyon Recreation Area (510-643-6720) and the Art Museum (510-642-0808) charge minimal fees.

GETTING THERE

➤ By car, from U.S. 80, take the University Ave. Exit. Continue to Oxford St. There's parking in public lots or on adjacent streets. About 20 minutes from U.S. 80.

➤ By public transit, take AC Transit buses F line (from San Francisco) or 7, 8, 9, 15, 40, 43, 51, 64, 65 or 67 (from East Bay). Or take BART to the Berkeley Downtown station and transfer to the U.C. Shuttle.

NEARBY

➤ Lawrence Hall of Science, Cal Performances, The Habitot, Hall of Health, Tilden Park, Berkeley Marina, Shoreline Park and Trail, Caesar Chavez Park.

COMMENT

➤ The university opens its doors to the public during Cal Day once a year in April. It includes events, entertainment, tours and the museums—all free. Plan a 3- to 4-hour visit.

The New Family Wonderland
YERBA BUENA GARDENS
AND THE METREON

Bordered by 4th, Mission, 3rd and Howard streets, San Francisco

The word has gotten out—San Francisco's new entertainment facility is a fabulous place for families. Convention goers bring your kids, they'll love the fun and educational activities. The Gardens feature a regulation-size ice rink, a 12-lane bowling center, a child development center, interactive play and learning gardens with a hedge maze and a historic carousel. Under the same roof is

Zeum—a cutting-edge art and technology center, theater and exhibition space where kids can create animation, produce multimedia art and learn about videography, puppetry, digital imaging and sound effects.

Across the street a family-friendly complex houses the Metreon—Sony's dazzling entertainment and shopping center. The Center for the Arts, an art gallery and a five-acre garden featuring an inspiring mixed-media memorial to Martin Luther King, Jr. are also located here. Metreon features the latest in entertainment technology. It boasts a 15-screen cinema, a 3-D IMAX™ theater and unique interactive attractions kids will want to visit again and again. Where the Wild Things Are, a life-size playland inspired by Maurice Sendak's charming book, enchants younger children. Older kids make a beeline to Airtight Garage, an interactive game zone based on the Moebius drawings of Jean Giraud. When your brood gets tired and hungry, the casual cafeteria-style restaurants serve tasty fare.

SEASONS AND TIMES
➤ These establishments keep regular business hours; call ahead for specific dates and times. Bowling and skating: (415) 777-3727. Metreon Entertainment Center: (415) 537-3400. Metreon: 1-800-METREON or www.metreon.com. Yerba Buena Center for the Arts: (415) 978-2787 Zeum: (415) 777-2800.

COST
➤ Free for the gardens, playground, maze and shopping center. The other venues charge fees.

GETTING THERE

➤ By car, from U.S. 80, take the 5th St. Exit and drive north to Mission St. Park at the 5th and Mission Street Garage. About 5 minutes from U.S. 80.

➤ By public transit, take Muni buses 9X, 30 or 45 to Yerba Buena Gardens. Or take the Muni Metro or BART to either the Powell or Montgomery stations.

NEARBY

➤ Museum of Modern Art, San Francisco Centre, Cartoon Art Museum.

COMMENT

➤ Check the calendar section of the newspaper for information on on-going exhibits, events and entertainment. Plan a 2- to 6-hour visit. Longer if you want to take in a movie.

CHAPTER 2

MUSEUMS

Introduction

Nowhere is the colorful history and character of the San Francisco Bay Area better captured than in its museums. San Francisco boasts a variety of outstanding institutions, and in this chapter you'll read about the ones that offer unique views of the city's special charm. Better still, these places have engaging hands-on displays, interactive exhibits, workshops and special programs where children can learn about local history, fire-fighting, art, transportation, Native culture, science and animals, and even how to draw cartoons. In visiting them you'll experience a wonderful blend of metropolis atmosphere and small-town hospitality. This is why San Francisco is such a great place for families.

See How They Run
CABLE CAR MUSEUM

1201 Mason St., San Francisco
(415) 474-1887
www.cablecarmuseum.com

What is the secret of cable car power? How do these Victorian antiques stay on their tracks while traveling San Francisco's steep hills? Find out at the Cable Car Museum where displays will answer these and other questions.

Hop on any San Francisco cable car and ask the conductor to let you off at the museum. It is located in the 1907 cable car barn and powerhouse on the edge of Chinatown. Here you will observe the clever system used to operate the cable cars. On the lower level of the barn, you can see four sets of cables that snake beneath San Francisco's streets. They run in a continuous circuit, pulling the cars along at about nine miles per hour. The huge revolving wheels guide the cables and make for fascinating viewing, as does the museum's 16-minute film covering the operation. Don't forget to check out the museum's display of antique model cable cars and gift shop.

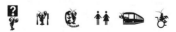

SEASONS AND TIMES
➤ Summer (Apr–Sept): Daily, 10 am–6 pm. Winter (Oct–Mar): Daily, 10 am–5 pm.

COST
➤ Free.

GETTING THERE
➤ By car, take The Embarcadero north to Bay St. and turn west. At Mason St. turn south and continue to the museum. Look for street parking. About 10 minutes from The Embarcadero.
➤ By public transit, take any cable car to the museum.
➤ On foot, from Grant St. in Chinatown, head west on Washington St. to Mason. The museum is on the corner. It's about a 15-minute walk from Grant.

NEARBY
➤ Chinatown.

COMMENT
➤ Plan a 2-hour visit. For delicious and inexpensive Chinese food after the visit, go to the Pot Sticker (150 Waverly Place), 1 block west of Grant.

The Art is the Draw
CALIFORNIA PALACE OF THE LEGION OF HONOR

**Legion of Honor Dr. at El Camino del Mar,
Lincoln Park, San Francisco
(415) 863-3330
www.thinker.org**

Here is a chance for your family to see an outstanding selection of famous art. The newly remodeled California Palace of the Legion of Honor really does look like a palace. Passing through the entrance of graceful columns, you are greeted by Rodin's famous sculpture, *The Thinker.* Inside, beautiful halls exhibit European paintings, sculptures, tapestries and furniture dating from medieval times.

Ask for the museum's pamphlet, then choose the highlights that you want to see in each hall such as Monet's famous *Water Lilies.* Engage your children as tour guides; have them help you find other paintings by Rubens, Rembrandt and Van Gogh.

On many Saturday afternoons, the museum offers one-hour programs to kids and parents. The sessions are free with your museum admission. You can read about the classes on page 111 of this book, or call (415-750-3658) for information.

After your visit, why not explore Lincoln Park where the museum is located? Its 270 acres feature high bluffs offering fantastic views of the Golden Gate Bridge. There are hiking trails that go for miles from San Francisco Headlands to Land's End near Cliff House.

SEASONS AND TIMES
➤ Year-round: Tue—Sun, 9:30 am—5 pm.

COST
➤ Adults $8, youths (12 to 17) $5, under 12 free. $2 off with Muni transfer. Free on second Wednesday of every month.

GETTING THERE
➤ By car, take U.S. 101 N. (Van Ness Ave.) to Geary St. Take Geary west to 34th Ave. and turn north (it becomes Legion of Honor Dr. in Lincoln Park). Free parking on site. About 20 minutes from Van Ness.
➤ By public transit, take Muni bus 18.

NEARBY
➤ Lincoln Park.

COMMENT
➤ The museum has a great café with outdoor dining on nice days and terrific views of the Pacific. Plan a 2-hour visit.

See You in the Funny Papers
CARTOON ART MUSEUM

814 Mission St., San Francisco
(415) 227-8666
www.cartoonart.org

If your kids enjoy cartoons—and what child doesn't—this place is perfect. The Cartoon Art Museum is the only museum of its kind on the West Coast and has all their favorites. Snoopy and Charlie Brown, Calvin and Hobbes, Batman, Dennis the Menace and Bugs Bunny are but a few. For connoisseurs, there is the work of William Hogarth and other early masters of the genre. Kids find the early comic strips and old-time popular characters like Prince Valiant strange, yet wonderful.

The museum displays comic books, as well as magazines, advertisements, animation drawing, and editorial and political cartoons. These form part of the 12,000-piece permanent collection. Don't head out before visiting the museum shop. It has an excellent selection of posters, original drawings and animation cels, along with cartoon books, mugs and T-shirts.

If your kids feel inspired to draw something, they might like to try cartooning. Classes are offered in the Children's Gallery at the nearby Metreon, where professional cartoonists show them how to draw popular characters and create their own. The sessions are two-and-a-half hours and the $35 fee includes all materials. When hunger strikes, the Metreon has casual restaurants with kid-friendly fare.

SEASONS AND TIMES
➤ Year-round: Wed—Fri, 11 am—5 pm; Sat, 10 am—5 pm; Sun 1—5 pm.

COST
➤ Adults $5, children (2 to 12) $2.

GETTING THERE
➤ By car, from I-80 N., take the Fremont St. Exit and drive to Howard St. Turn west on Howard continuing to 5th St. Turn north to the Fifth and Mission Parking Garage. About 10 minutes from the freeway exit.
➤ By public transit, take BART or Muni Metro lines J, K, L, M or N to the Montgomery or Powell Street stations. Or take Muni buses 5, 9, 14, 15, 30, 38 or 45.

NEARBY
➤ Yerba Buena Center for the Arts, Metreon, Zeum, San Francisco Museum of Modern Art.

COMMENT
➤ Not all cartoons may be suitable for children, parents should take a quick look through the exhibits beforehand. Plan a 1-hour visit.

Up, Up and Away
HILLER MUSEUM OF AVIATION

**601 Skyway Rd., San Carlos
(650) 654-0200
www.hiller.org**

The Hiller Museum of Aviation is a walk through 100 years of flying machines, from the most primitive to the futuristic. Its collection of aircraft, models, interactive displays and multimedia presentations are designed to inspire enthusiasts of all ages with an educational and entertaining look at aviation history.

The museum's finely crafted aircraft (some are full-scale replicas, others the real thing) recount aviation's amazing tales, from its beginnings in Europe and Northern California in the early 1800s to the present day. Currently, the museum has over 75 aircraft, including civilian and military planes and futuristic models designed for vertical take-off and landing. A few of the planes are set up for visitors to enter and explore. In the 5,000-square-foot workshop, giant windows let you watch staff carefully restore the latest acquisitions.

The Flight Store is paradise for anyone who's fascinated with flight. It has a huge collection of toys, books, flight apparel, models and memorabilia. Be prepared to buy a souvenir to take home.

For a special thrill, check out the Young Eagles flights. On the third Saturday of every month, children ages eight and up can go for a ride in a plane with an experienced pilot.

SEASONS AND TIMES
➤ Year-round: Daily, 10 am—5 pm. Closed Easter, Thanksgiving, Christmas and New Year's.

COST
➤ Adults $7, youths (8 to 17), under 7 free with an adult. Young Eagles flights are free.

GETTING THERE
➤ By car, take U.S. 101 S. to the Holly St./Redwood Shores Pkwy. Exit. Go east onto Redwood Shores until Airport Rd. Turn south to Skyway Rd. Free parking on site. About 25 minutes from downtown.

NEARBY
➤ Coyote Point Park, Museum for Environmental Education.

COMMENT
➤ There is no café, but the museum has vending machines with snacks and drinks. Plan a 1.5-hour visit.

Discovering the Past
MARIN MUSEUM OF THE AMERICAN INDIAN

**2200 Novato Blvd., Novato
(415) 897-4064
www.Marinindian.com**

L
ong before Europeans settled around San Francisco, local tribes of Native Americans lived and thrived in the Bay Area. The Marin Museum of the American Indian located in Miwok Park, offers visitors a glimpse of their fascinating world and culture.

Kids will be most interested in the exhibit in the museum's main gallery. Tools, Toys and Treasures of Native North Americans reveals the toys children played with long ago. They'll also view cooking utensils women used to prepare the family dinner and see striking ceremonial masks and other interesting treasures. Another exhibit hall has an education wall with a series of hands-on displays kids can operate to learn more about what foods Native Americans ate, how they built their homes and what they made their clothes from. Some of the museum's staff is Native American, and are delighted to share interesting stories with children and explain some of the customs and folklore.

After the indoor visit, head outside. The spacious park surrounding the museum has lots of room to run and play. A redwood grove, Native and medicinal gardens and a kotcha (a replica of a redwood log house) can be explored.

SEASONS AND TIMES
→ Year-round: Tue—Fri, 10 am—3 pm. Closed Easter, Thanksgiving, Christmas, and New Year's.

COST
→ Adults $7, youths (8 to 17) $5, under 7 free with an adult.

GETTING THERE
→ By car, take U.S. 101 N. to the DeLong Ave. Exit. Drive west to Novato Blvd. Turn south and continue for a little over a mile to Miwok Park and the museum. Free parking on site. About 50 minutes from downtown.

NEARBY
→ Point Reyes National Seashore, Bear Valley.

COMMENT
→ This is a great place to go for a short walk to explore the creek and redwood grove. Bring a picnic lunch since the museum does not have a café. Plan a 2-hour visit.

California Dreaming
OAKLAND MUSEUM
OF CALIFORNIA

**1000 Oak St., Oakland
(510) 238-2200, (888) 625-6873
or (510) 238-3818 (Family Explorations!)
www.museumca.org**

A short trip across the Bay Bridge takes you to the Oakland Museum of California. With three tiers of galleries interspersed with gardens, courts and terraces, the museum is a fun and interesting place for kids to explore. They will discover an exceptional array of interactive exhibits on everything California—history, art, environment, diversity and culture.

Enticing walk-about displays put you in the world of the Gold Rush with early Native Americans, missions and ranchos. You'll also experience the great earthquake of 1906, the Summer of Love in the 60s and Silicon Valley today. A theme-based exhibit hall allows you to walk across the state—from the rugged Sierra Nevada desert to the Pacific coast—as it was hundreds of years ago. Other galleries depict California's natural aquatic beauty with displays on its ocean environments, rivers, streams and unique estuaries.

Family Explorations! is a popular program helping parents or grandparents explore the museum with kids. It features live performances and work-on-art projects to take home.

SEASONS AND TIMES
➤ Year-round: Wed—Sat, 10 am—5 pm; Sun, noon—5 pm. First Friday of every month, 10 am—9 pm.

COST
➤ Adults $6, children (6 to 17) $4.

GETTING THERE
➤ By car, take I-80 E. to the Oak St. Exit. Head east on Oak to 10th St. There's pay parking in the garage under the museum. About 35 minutes from downtown.
➤ By public transit, take BART to Lake Merritt Station. Or take AC Transit buses 14, 15, 36X, 43, 40, 11 or 62.

NEARBY
➤ Jack London Square, Oakland Estuary, USS *Potomac*, USS *Hornet* Museum, Lake Merritt, Children's Fairyland.

COMMENT
➤ The museum's café has delicious kid-friendly food. Plan a 2-hour visit.

Pumpers, Steamers and Musters!
PIONEER MEMORIAL FIRE MUSEUM

**San Francisco Fire Department, Station 10 Annex,
655 Presidio Ave., San Francisco
(415) 558-3546
www.sffiremuseum.org**

Fire Station 10 is a working fire hall and home to the Pioneer Memorial Fire Museum. One of San Francisco's truly unique museums, its collection of fire-fighting equipment is among the most comprehensive in the United States. The museum is a fascinating place for families and fire-fighting buffs.

Some of the amazing exhibit pieces, such as hose tenders, steamers, hand pumps and fire bells, date back to the Gold Rush when San Francisco's population exploded from a few hundred people to over 30,000. The "tent and shack metropolis" as the makeshift city was called, burned to the ground six times between 1849 and 1851. This prompted the formation of volunteer fire-fighting companies such as the St. Francis Hook & Ladder Society. Today the society is the official historical body of the San Francisco Fire Department and oversees the Fire Museum.

Besides ogling the array of equipment (volunteers explain how the pieces work), kids can check out the five-minute video of a muster, with hose cart pulls, hand pumper contests and horse drawn steamers in action. Don't forget to browse the gift store. It's stocked with unusual fire-fighting-related souvenirs appropriate for every age.

SEASONS AND TIMES
➤ Year-round: Thu—Sun, 1—4 pm. Closed all major holidays.

COST
➤ Free.

GETTING THERE
➤ By car, take U.S. 101 N. (Van Ness Ave.) to Geary St. Turn west on Geary to Presidio Ave. and drive north. Street parking available. About 15 minutes from Van Ness.
➤ By public transit, take Muni buses 1AX, 1BX, 31, 38 or 43.

NEARBY
➤ Golden Gate Park, Presidio, Golden Gate National Recreation Area, Marina Greens, Japantown.

COMMENT
➤ You can see the museum's colorful, historic apparatus in operation in San Francisco parades and special events. Plan a 1-hour visit.

A *Hidden Treasure*
RANDALL MUSEUM

199 Museum Way, San Francisco
(415) 554-9600
www.randallmuseum.org/

The Randall Museum is a cornerstone in the lives of many San Franciscans—for good reason. The museum has a strong commitment to educating and entertaining children with engaging hands-on exhibits, nature and art classes, and programs for families.

Parents are awestruck with the spectacular city views from the Randall's hilltop perch. Children are just as taken with the displays inside. They can examine minerals and glittering gems, handle dinosaur bones, perform experiments in chemistry and biology labs and more. In a unique area called Make-a-Quake, kids are required to jump up and down to create "seismic force." A favorite feature is the live animal room where they'll learn first-hand about owls, snakes, mice and raccoons. The youngest in your brood will enjoy petting the ducks and rabbits in the small animal corral.

There's always something interesting happening at the Randall, including the popular Saturday drop-in workshops with planned activities and the occasional field trip to explore local animals and geography. Make sure you request a copy of the museum's current schedule of events.

SEASONS AND TIMES
➤ Year-round: Tue—Sat, 10 am—5 pm. Animal talks: Sat, 11 am.

COST
➤ Donations accepted. There are fees for some programs.

GETTING THERE
➤ By car, take Market St. southwest to 17th St. and head west on 17th. Turn north at Roosevelt and continue until Museum Way and drive east. Free parking on site. About 15 minutes from Market St.
➤ By public transit, take Muni buses 24 or 37.

NEARBY
➤ Corona Park, Buena Vista Park, Golden Gate Park.

COMMENT
➤ Just down the hill on Haight St., you can order takeout from several good restaurants and eat it at nearby Corona Park. Plan a 2- to 3-hour visit.

State-of-the-art
SAN FRANCISCO MUSEUM OF MODERN ART

**151 – 3rd St., San Francisco
(415) 357-4000 (Museum) or (415) 357-4097
(Family Programs)
www.sfmoma.org**

C hildren need not know a thing about abstract expressionism to enjoy the San Francisco Museum of Modern Art, or SFMOMA as it's called.

Now second only in size to New York's Museum of Modern of Art, SFMOMA's stunning new building is spacious, bright and features a 145-foot-tall skylight tower. The building itself is considered a main attraction and is a spectacular setting for viewing art. The museum's frequently changing exhibits are a great way to introduce kids to the modern masters. The bright colors and interesting shapes created by such impressionist and modern painters as Matisse, Picasso, Klee, Rivera and for a touch of surrealism, Salvador Dali, appeal to children as much as adults. Feeling creative? SFMOMA's Family Sundays, held at the Koret Education Center from noon to 3 pm, offer kids the chance to attend hands-on-art-making sessions in a studio. The classes are free and directed by guest artists.

Don't overlook the Museum store. It has a superb selection of art books, supplies and prints. Kids love exploring the children's section with its instructional books and educational toys, many of which can be tried on the spot.

SEASONS AND TIMES
➙ Summer (Memorial Day—Labor Day): Fri—Tue, 10 am—6 pm; Thu, 10 am—9 pm. Winter (Labor Day—Memorial Day): Fri—Tue, 11 am—6 pm; Thu, 11 am—9 pm. Closed July 4, Thanksgiving, Christmas and New Year's.

COST
➙ Individuals $9, children (12 and under) free.

GETTING THERE
➙ By car, take I-80. From East Bay, exit at Fremont St. Turn southwest onto Howard St. Drive for 2 blocks and turn north onto 3rd St. From South or North Bay, exit at 4th St. which leads onto Bryant. Continue on Bryant to 3rd and turn north to the museum.

Park in the Fifth and Mission Garage. About 10 minutes from the
freeway exit.
➤ By public transit, take BART or Muni Metro lines J, K, L, M or N
to the Montgomery or Powell street stations. Or take Muni buses 5,
9, 14, 30, 38 or 45.

NEARBY
➤ Yerba Buena Center for the Arts, Metreon, Zeum, Cartoon
Museum.

COMMENT
➤ SFMOMA's Caffe Museo has convenient, yummy snacks and
light meals. Plan a 1- to 2-hour visit.

Gold Rush Fever
WELLS FARGO HISTORY MUSEUM

420 Montgomery St., San Francisco
(415) 396-2619
www.WellsFargohistory.com

G old nuggets the size of your fist? Stagecoaches?
A telegraph machine that sends messages?
This is the stuff kids dream of. Take them to the
lobby in the Wells Fargo Bank in the San Francisco
Financial District and they slip back 150 years to the days
of the California Gold Rush.

In the late 1800s, Wells Fargo operated the Pony
Express mail delivery service and 10-passenger
stagecoaches in the Great Overland Mail Route from
San Francisco to Missouri. The displays, some are
hands-on, recount that exciting era in the company's

history during those frontier days. Kids can climb onto a cutaway stagecoach seat, hold the reins and pretend to outrun the famous bandit-poet, Black Bart. Or squeeze everyone into another coach to experience the cramped, stuffy accommodations Wells Fargo passengers endured. Walk through the recreated Wells Fargo office and see a working telegraph, an agent's desk with documents, treasure boxes and scales. The general store doubles as a gift shop and has interesting souvenirs related to the Gold Rush, from gold-panning kits and piggy banks, to model stage coaches and parchment imitations of musty, old documents.

SEASONS AND TIMES
➤ Year-round: Mon—Fri, 9 am—5 pm.

COST
➤ Free.

GETTING THERE
➤ By car, the museum is located in the heart of the downtown Financial District. Parking when found is expensive.
➤ By public transit, take any of the Muni buses (Market St. lines) to Montgomery St. Or take the Muni Metro to the Montgomery Street Station. If you take the cable car (California St.), the museum is about a 15-minute walk north on Montgomery.

NEARBY
➤ Chinatown, Embarcadero Center, Justin Herman Plaza.

COMMENT
➤ Stairs only lead to the second floor exhibits. You'll find family-friendly places to eat in Chinatown, Embarcadero Center and Justin Herman Plaza. Plan a 1-hour visit.

CHAPTER 3

IN YOUR NEIGHBORHOOD

Introduction

You don't need to travel far in the Bay Area to find attractions and activities that interest kids. Some of the best places are in your own neighborhood and are free or low-cost.

This chapter includes a variety of ideas for outings—farmers' markets, ceramic painting studios, ice rinks, bowling alleys and other everyday places where a little imagination can turn an ordinary trip into a fun-filled adventure. This chapter also tells you about one of the best sources for free entertainment—local libraries, which often offer storytelling, craft and drama programs in addition to their collections.

The following listings introduce you to the possibilities for family fun in your neck of the woods and invite you to explore other neighborhoods. You'll find a few specific suggestions to get you started and places where you can find more information.

Also, a wealth of information on the Internet—http://bayarea.citysearch.com has general information. At www.guideyou.com, www.viamagazine.com, www.gocalif.com and www.chronicleevents.com, you'll find details on current events throughout the area and listings for individual topics.

Don't forget the free regional parenting newspapers—a valuable resource you find at libraries, cafés and bookstores. *Bay Area Parent* (www.parenthood web.com) prints several editions targeting different locales. *Parents' Press* (www.parentspress.com) has a strong East Bay focus. *Sonoma Parents* (www.the parentsjournal.com) also contains information devoted to families.

Rainy Day
BOWLING ALLEYS

Over the years, bowling has lost some of its glitter as an essential American pastime. That message, however, hasn't reached kids who still take delight in knocking down pins and keeping score. Bowling is a great outing for children of all ages and parents. Even toddlers will have fun rolling the ball—albeit playing by their own rules. More than just fun, it's inexpensive (around $1 to $3 a game per person, plus shoe rental). Most alleys offer instruction, leagues for players of all ages and often host special and seasonal events—Halloween Bowling, Mom's Night Out, and Dad and Me to name a few. Birthday party packages are also available at many bowling alleys.

If you have older children, a regular lane and a lightweight ball are all you need for a roaring good time. If your family includes smaller children, consider a game of bumper bowling. Most Bay Area bowling centers have gutter pads, and some lanes have built-in fold-back rails that enable even the youngest bowler to get the ball to the pins. Call before you head out to find out what family activities are on the menu, or to get off-hour specials. Here are the names of a few family-friendly bowling centers to get you started.

ALBANY BOWL
540 San Pablo Ave., Albany
(510) 526-8818

AMF SOUTHSHORE LANES
300 Park Blvd., Alameda
(510) 523-6767

JAPANTOWN BOWL
Post St. and Webster St., San Francisco
(415) 921-6200

YERBA BUENA ICE SKATING & BOWLING CENTER
750 Folsom St., San Francisco
(415) 777-3727

Local Treasure Chests
CHILDREN'S LIBRARIES

V isit any public library in the Bay Area and you'll find a section devoted to children. These days they contain more than books and cozy corners. Your kids will have access to games, toys, music, interactive computers and Internet facilities. Libraries have Spanish/English bilingual story times for toddlers, preschoolers and families, book clubs and many special events and activities for children throughout the year. Summer programs feature free shows by noted children's entertainers and free workshops with instruction in crafts, drama, science and other fun topics. The theme changes each summer, but programs always include prizes for kids who reach their reading goals.

There are municipal and/or county library systems throughout the Bay Area, each with their own collections, programs and hours. Check the government listings in your local phone book for information on those nearest you. In most cases, kids can get their own library cards and borrow books, videos, CDs and magazines for up to three weeks. And, at most libraries, there are no overdue fines on children's material checked out by kids or adults. If there is a particular item you want that your library doesn't have, ask the reference librarians. They can usually get it for you on interlibrary loan.

The Fun Never Stops at COMMUNITY CENTERS AROUND THE BAY

You don't have to go far in any direction to find some kind of preschool, after school or vacation program. Municipal park and recreation departments are a natural place to start. While a sandbox and jungle gym are often more than enough for toddlers, older children find that the City of San Francisco (415-831-2700; http://parks.sfgov.org/) offers all kinds of athletic leagues—from table tennis to flag football—as well as socializing activities for "tiny tots." Latchkey kids programs are also offered and there's Friday night entertainment.

You can find listings for many of the public programs in your local phone book. The ads in parenting newspapers (see chapter introduction) are a good source for commercial programs. In addition to the basics, you'll find listings for gymnastics classes, climbing walls, every kind of athletic activity, art, dance, music, theater, cooking, sewing classes—in short just about any structured activity that is fun for kids.

Party Central
COSTUMES, SUPPLIES AND INVITES

Picture aisle after aisle of wigs, boas, glitter, gowns, hero garb, popular character masks, false whiskers and full-body costumes. Kids have a ball with all the funny objects from clown noses to paste-on scars. Whether you are looking to add to your family's dress-up box or throw the perfect party, several Bay Area merchants stand ready to help you turn your dream persona and party into a reality.

You'll find listings for lots of costume shops online at http://bayarea.citysearch.com/. Some of these establishments offer professional costumes, others focus on adult dress-up and a few are specialized boutiques. For instance, one shop is devoted to Carnaval costumes. Call ahead and ask what items the store carries. In addition to lots of costumes, most stores have a full range of party supplies. Also look in the yellow pages for dozens of other possibilities under the headings for "Party Supplies and/or Costumes." Below are a few to check out.

HOUSE OF HUMOR
747 El Camino Real, Redwood City
(650) 368-5524

HOUSE OF MAGIC
2025 Chestnut St., San Francisco
(415) 346-2218

STAGECRAFT STUDIOS
1854 Alcatraz Ave., Berkeley
(510) 653-4424

Fresh Produce
FARMERS' MARKETS

Low on groceries? Why not make your next outing for family staples an entertaining and educational adventure. The Bay Area's farmers' markets offer you the chance to do that—purchase fruits, vegetables and other products direct from the growers, and talk to them about their work. No doubt your kids will learn to appreciate fresh food for its beauty, superior taste and healthy qualities.

While the prices are usually about the same as those you would pay at the store, the freshness and quality of the produce and the open-air market atmosphere make shopping at a supermarket pale in comparison.

You'll find listings for a few of the larger and more centrally located farmers' markets in the Bay Area on page 124. However, these are just the beginning. A more extensive list produced by the California Federation of Certified Farmers Markets is found online at http://farmersmarket.ucdavis.edu/. County agricultural commissioners approve the establishments appearing on the list. Certified farmers sell only agricultural products they grow themselves.

Skate Away the Day
ICE RINKS

I s your family intent on gliding the hours away? Thanks to modern technology, at Christmas time you can take the gang skating outdoors in San Francisco. Ice-making equipment, brought in especially for the holidays, keeps the ice surface hard and fast at the outdoor rink on The Embarcadero at the foot of Market Street. Kids and adults can't help but imagine they are somewhere more northerly (or easterly) as they cut their turns.

For the rest of the year, kids settle for practicing their twirling or getting ice hockey lessons at an indoor rink. Snow and ice are foreign to the Bay Area, but local rinks are always a hit. Below are the names of some of the popular arenas in the area. Most feature lessons, hockey leagues, special family skate sessions and birthday party packages.

BELMONT ICELAND
815 Old County Rd., Belmont
(650) 592-4338

BERKELEY ICELAND
2727 Milvia St., Berkeley
(510) 647-1600

ICE CHALET
2202 Bridgepointe Pkwy., San Mateo
(650) 574-1616

OAKLAND ICE CENTER
519 – 18th St., Oakland
(510) 269-9000

YERBA BUENA ICE SKATING & BOWLING CENTER
750 Folsom St., San Francisco
(415) 777-3727

Places to
PAINT YOUR OWN POTTERY

I f your kids need a new medium for expressing their artistic ability, take them to a ceramics studio to paint pottery. You can purchase cups, bowls, piggy banks, vases, picture frames and other assorted knickknacks. The studio supplies the paints, brushes, stencils, sponges and helpful hints to keep your kids busy creating masterpieces. Some studios charge by the hour in addition to the cost of the items, which start at about $5. Younger children tend to finish their projects quickly, so it's a good idea to put a limit on the number of pieces they can paint or this activity will become expensive.

Paint-your-own-pottery studios are also a great idea for birthday parties and field trips. Some studios have separate rooms that can be reserved for groups. When you've finished your art, the studio will have the finished pieces glazed and fired in about a week. Below are the names of a couple of popular pottery painting establishments. For a studio near you, check the telephone book under "Ceramics."

BRUSHSTROKES STUDIO
745 Page St., Berkeley
(206) 329-1604

COLOR ME MINE
2030 Union St., San Francisco
(415) 474-7076

Cool Places to Play
SWIMMING POOLS

The best place to cool off on hot summer days (or warm up on a winter day) is at your local pool. Community pools (indoor and outdoor) offer swimming lessons for children of all ages. Other aquatic sports and lifesaving instruction are also available. Many pools have swimming sessions for families, classes for parents and tots and special events for kids. Some pools have party rooms you can rent for birthdays.

The San Francisco Recreation and Park Department (415-831-2700; http://parks.sfgov.org) has nine pools scattered throughout the city. Lessons, as well as recreational and lap swimming, are offered. Check your local or neighboring municipalities to see what kind of facilities are available. YMCAs in San Francisco, Marin, Berkeley and Oakland have pools that are available to members and for drop-in use. Prices vary by location.

East Bay residents have two wonderful choices for swimming in addition to their community pools. The Richmond Plunge (1 E. Richmond Ave., Richmond, 510-620-6820) features a huge, renovated 1920s pool—originally filled with saltwater from the Bay—plus wading pool and fountain. The Strawberry Canyon Recreational Area in Berkeley, a facility of the University of California (Centennial Dr., 510-643-6720) is available for community use at a small fee. It's an outdoor pool in a beautiful setting, but is closed during winter.

CHAPTER 4

PLACES TO PLAY

Introduction

I f it were left up to kids, they'd play all day long. Fortunately for them, the Bay Area is ringed with parks, amusement centers and other wonderful destinations where fun is the number one priority. Great America features a lively mix of entertaining shows, costumed characters, animal exhibits and amusement rides. Children's Fairyland keeps youngsters spellbound as their favorite tales come to life. This chapter describes some of the most visited favorites. You can find many others close to home by checking your local parks and recreation department listings in the telephone book. Then make your plans. Days of fun await you.

The Heart of the Action
BERKELEY MARINA

The foot of University Ave. (west of I-80), Berkeley
www.berkeley.gov.ca.us

Berkeley Marina invites you to step into a world of pleasant pursuits. How do fishing, kite flying, biking and in-line skating along the Bay sound? Perhaps you prefer sailing or kayaking? Berkeley Marina Bait and Tackle Shop (510-849-2727) can outfit you for fishing, and boat rentals are available at the Berkeley Marina Sport Center (510-849-2727). Or, take the family walking 3,000 feet into the Bay on the Berkeley Pier for stunning views of San Francisco, Angel Island, Alcatraz and Mount Tamalpais.

Hours of constructive fun await kids at Adventure Playground (510-644-8623). They can build a playhouse, add to one of the structures in progress, paint their own wood-crafted creation and more. Later, drop by the Shorebird Nature Center (510-644-6376, ext. 4). It has live exhibits and ecology-related activities for kids. The grassy park features a small beach.

If you hike out to North Waterfront, bring your kite. It's always windy here and people gather to practice their stunt kite skills. The new shoreline trail—paved for biking, skating, or pushing a stroller—stretches miles north along the Bay from the Berkeley Marina to Point Richmond with million-dollar views along the way.

SEASONS AND TIMES
➛ Year-round: Daily, 8 am—sunset.

COST
➛ Free. Fees for rentals.

GETTING THERE
➛ By car, from downtown, take I-80 E. across the Bay Bridge and head north on I-80 towards Vallejo and Sacramento. Take the University Ave. Exit. This will put you on University Ave. heading east. Turn south on 6th St. Go around the block and access University heading west. Cross over the freeway and continue west to the Marina. Free parking on site. About 15 minutes from downtown.
➛ By public transit, take BART to the Downtown Berkeley station. Transfer to AC Transit line bus 51 and ride it to the Berkeley Marina.

NEARBY
➛ U.C. Berkeley campus, Lawrence Hall of Science, Tilden Park.

COMMENT
➛ Bring sunscreen, jackets and water bottles for outdoor activities. There is a snack bar at the bait shop and restaurant/deli at the foot of University. Buy fixings for a picnic lunch and plan to spend the afternoon. H's Lorships (510-843-2733) and Skates on the Bay (510-549-1900), two restaurants on Seawall Dr. (at the edge of the Bay on the Marina) have kids' menus. Reservations recommended.

Stepping Through the Looking Glass
CHILDREN'S FAIRYLAND

**699 Bellevue Ave., Oakland
(510) 238-6876 or (510) 238-6877 (Birthday parties)
www.fairyland.org**

This historic outdoor park has enchanted families for five decades. It brings beloved children's stories to life through exhibits, animals and Talking Storybooks that kids activate using a "Magic Key." Thirty colorful sets over ten acres depict the make-believe world of *Alice in Wonderland*, *Captain Hook*, *Goldilocks* and other favorite fairy tales and nursery rhymes. Daily puppet shows, performances by Fairyland Personalities, "small folk" rides and special programs including magic shows, storytelling and music are all part of the Fairyland experience.

Maybe one of your children would like to become a Fairyland Personality for a season. Kids (ages eight to ten) can audition for one of the roles. Children's Fairyland was America's first three-dimensional storybook theme park. It was so successful, Walt Disney personally asked the director to help him develop his plan for an amusement park for families.

SEASONS AND TIMES
➤ Apr 1—June 17: Wed—Sun, 10 am—4 pm. June 18—Sept 3: Daily, 10 am—4:30 pm. Sept 5—Oct: Wed—Sun, 10 am—4 pm. Oct—Apr 1: Fri—Sun, 10 am—4 pm.

COST
➤ Individuals $5, under 1 free. Price includes unlimited rides.

GETTING THERE
➤ By car, from downtown, take I-80 E. over the Bay Bridge. After the bridge merge onto I-580 E. Take the Grand Ave. Exit and head southwest to Bellevue Ave. and follow the "Children's Fairyland" signs. Street parking only. About 20 minutes from downtown.

NEARBY
➤ Lake Merritt, Rotary Nature Center, Oakland Museum.

COMMENT
➤ This is a charming place for birthday parties. Adults cannot enter without a child. Plan a 2- to 3-hour visit.

Bustin' Loose
THE CHILDREN'S PLAYGROUND AT GOLDEN GATE PARK

**Bordered by The Great Highway, Fulton St., Stanyan St. and Lincoln Way, San Francisco
(415) 391-2000
http://parks.sfgov.org**

Make sure the Children's Playground is on your must-see list when visiting Golden Gate Park (page 22). Located on Lincoln

Avenue on the southeast side of the park, the play area is spruced up and features an assortment of new—and kids will think—cool play structures. All ages enjoy zooming down several different slides. The playground also boasts play structures for climbing. One of them has fascinating geometrical shapes and is handicapped accessible.

Surrounding the play area is a level grassy field that's perfect for throwing a Frisbee™ or ball, or doing cartwheels and somersaults. Nearby, a perfectly restored Herschell-Spillman carousel, dating from the early 1900s, sports 62 animals in pairs from cats and dogs, to tigers, reindeer and frogs. Or spin until you're pleasantly giddy in the carousel's love-tub.

SEASONS AND TIMES
➤ Park and playground: Year-round, daily. Carousel: Year-round, daily, 10 am–4:30 pm. McClaren Lodge and Park Headquarters (415-831-2700) is open weekdays.

COST
➤ Park and playground: Free. Carousel: Adults $1.50, children $0.25.

GETTING THERE
➤ By car, from U.S. 101 (Van Ness Ave.), take Fell St. west to the park entrance on John F. Kennedy Dr. Free parking on site. About 20 minutes from U.S. 101.
➤ By public transit, Muni buses 5, 6, 7, 16AX, BX, 28, 29, 44, 66 and 71 all stop here. Or, take the Muni Metro (N-Judah line).

NEARBY
➤ California Academy of Sciences, Steinhart Aquarium, Morrison Planetarium. Asian Art Museum.

COMMENT
➤ Plan a 2-hour visit, longer for the park's other attractions.

Whooping it Up
GREAT AMERICA

Great America Pkwy., Santa Clara
(408) 988-1776
www.pgathrills.com

No two ways about it, excitement and fun await at Great America. Northern California's largest family amusement park offers its share of thrill rides, such as hair-raising roller coasters and gravity-defying attractions. But the park features tamer rides, too. Take younger children in your group to Kidzville. It comprises a large section of the park and features dozens of scaled-down, gentle rides and activities that kids and parents can do together.

Nickelodeon Splat City is a recent and very popular addition to Great America. Kids get to meet the Rugrats™ characters and splash through a giant water maze. Still on the watery theme, nothing beats summer's heat quicker than the River Rafting Adventure. It takes you plunging through drenching, cooling waves. There are loads of carney games at Great America—wouldn't it make a little one's day to win a larger-than-life stuffed animal? Or how about letting your young ones drive you for a change —in an antique roadster. When you need a break, there's music, comedians and other live entertainment. IMAX™ films are presented, too. Or take the gang in the aerial tram and let them see the action unfolding below. At ground level, unwind in one of the park's many cafés.

SEASONS AND TIMES
➤ Summer (Memorial Day—Labor Day): Sun—Fri, 10 am—9 pm; Sat, 10 am—11 pm. March: Sat—Sun, 10 am—7 pm.

COST
➤ Individuals (7 to 59) $32.99, children (3 to 6) $19.99, under 3 free.

GETTING THERE
➤ By car, from downtown, take U.S. 101 S. (Van Ness Ave.) to the Great American Pkwy. Exit and follow the signs. Pay parking on site ($6). About 45 minutes from downtown.

COMMENT
➤ Bring sunscreen, towels and a change of clothes for after the water maze and rafting ride. Vendors sell all the food kids love, but it's expensive. Bring your own lunch and store it in lockers at the park entrance. With the high cost of admission, plan to spend the day.

A *Hi-tech Playground*
MALIBU GRAND PRIX
AND MALIBU CASTLE

320 and 340 Blomquist St., Redwood City
(650) 367-1906 (Malibu Castle)
(650) 366-6463 (Malibu Grand Prix)
www.malibugrandprix.com

Malibu Grand Prix and Malibu Castle, actually one entertainment park, cater to families with kids of various ages. For many visitors the highlight is the miniature golf. Malibu Castle features three 18-hole courses with challenging obstacles (including lagoons). Baseball and softball players aren't forgotten. The Castle has eight batting cages where everyone enjoys a turn at bat. Ball speeds range from 30 to 85 miles per hour with bats and helmets provided. You'll find lots of arcade games, as well as prize games (win tickets and take home a prize) and air-hockey. When hunger strikes—and it will—the on-site pizza parlor has kids' favorite toppings.

Feel like laying down a little rubber? At Malibu Grand Prix, up-and-coming racers (and parents) strap themselves into custom-built 3/4 scale Indy-style cars and zoom around a twisting, turning 1/2-mile track. Drivers must be 42 inches or taller. Those with the thrill of racing in their blood (and at least 56 inches tall) can try the F-50 racecar.

SEASONS AND TIMES
➤ Year-round: Sun—Thu, 10 am—10 pm; Fri—Sat, 10 am—midnight.

COST
➤ Grand Prix: $3.50 per lap. Malibu Golf: Adults $6, under 13 $5.50; Early-bird (10 am—11 am) $3. Games: 4 tokens for $1.

GETTING THERE
➤ By car, from downtown, take U.S. 101 S. (Van Ness Ave.) to the Seaport Blvd./Woodside Rd. Exit. Stay left at the fork and take Seaport Blvd. eastbound. Turn north at the blinking red stop light onto Blomquist St. Malibu Grand Prix is the first driveway on the west side of Blomquist. Malibu Castle is a bit further on the same side. Free parking on site. About 30 minutes from downtown.

COMMENT
➤ The Castle has a well-equipped room for birthday parties (packages include miniature golf, game tokens, pizza, ice cream and drinks). Most activities are outdoors—wear sunscreen. Plan a 2- to 3-hour visit.

Play all Day
THE PLAYGROUND AT MOUNTAIN LAKE PARK

Lake St. (Funston Ave. to 8th Ave.), San Francisco
(415) 831-2700
http://parks.sfgov.org

A double dose of adventure awaits visitors at Mountain Lake Park. First there are the attractions in the park, including the picturesque Mountain Lake. It's perfect for skipping stones and watching wildlife (swimming and fishing are not permitted in the lake). You'll find lots of grassy meadows for playing games, shaded walkways, jogging trails, a batting cage and courts for tennis and basketball.

The park's playground is the biggest draw for young families and is a kid's paradise. The multi-tiered play area features a full complement of swings, colorful climbing structures, slides and lots of sand for soft landings and scooping with sand toys. Don't forget the pails and shovels. Bring everyone's bike and in-line skates, too. Mountain Lake Park borders on the historic Presidio. The Spanish built the Presidio as a military base in the late 1700s. Later the U.S. Army used it. Today the Presidio is part of the Golden Gate National Recreation Area offering park go'ers miles of paved trails, forested groves, military buildings, gun installations and spectacular views of the Golden Gate.

SEASONS AND TIMES
→ Year-round: Daily, 6 am—9 pm.

COST
→ Free.

GETTING THERE
→ By car, take U.S. 101 (Van Ness Ave.) to Geary St. Turn west on Geary to 8th Ave. and turn north to Mountain Lake Park. Free parking on site. About 20 minutes from U.S.101.
→ By public transit, take Muni buses 44, 28, or 28L to Mountain Lake Park.

NEARBY
↦ The Presidio, Fort Point, Palace of Legion of Honor.

COMMENT
↦ This is a great place for picnics. There are lots of tables and grassy areas to spread a blanket. Plan a 2- to 3-hour visit.

Big Park Thrills
SIX FLAGS MARINE WORLD

2001 Marine World Pkwy., Vallejo
(707) 644-4000
www.sixflags.com

Six Flags Marine World is America's only combination wildlife park, oceanarium and theme park. One entrance fee entitles you to see it all—more than 30 amusement rides, 35 animal attractions, 10 super shows, 2 play areas and Looney Toons Seaport. This is a park within a park for families with young children.

Make Seaport your first stop if youngsters are in your group. This kiddie playland has ten tame rides and two interactive play zones. If that's not enough, there's the Bugs Bunny's musical revue, *What's Up, Rock?* and personality characters—Bugs Bunny, Daffy Duck, Sylvester, Tweety and Tasmanian Devil—to greet the kids. To see real animals, steer the gang to Marine World. It houses more than 3,000 creatures, including some pretty unusual ones such as penguins from tropical Africa. Marine World also runs a sea lion breeding program. Kids can come face to face with tame barnyard animals at the ever-popular Petting Paddock. Batman fans will want to visit Gotham Harbor, where Batman and Robin take time to meet guests in between Batman Water Thrill Spectacular shows.

SEASONS AND TIMES
➤ Spring Break (Apr) and Memorial Day–Labor Day: Mon–Fri, 10 am–8 pm; Sat–Sun, 10 am–10 pm. Spring and Fall: Fri–Sun, 10 am–8 pm. Call (707) 643-ORCA (6722) for information on tickets and operating hours, subject to change with the weather.

COST
➤ Individuals (13 and up) $34, children (4 to 12) $17, under 4 free.

GETTING THERE
➤ By car, from downtown, take I-80 E. across the Bay Bridge. Continue north on I-80 towards Vallejo and Sacramento. The park is located on the northeast side of Vallejo next to the county fairgrounds, just off I-80. Free parking on site. From U.S. 101 S. take the Great American Pkwy. Exit and follow the signs. About 45 minutes from downtown.

COMMENT
➤ Bring sunscreen, towels and a change of clothes in case your kids get wet on the Monsoon Falls or White Water Safari rides. Vendors sell all the food kids love, but it's expensive. Bring your own lunch and store it in lockers at the park entrance. With the high cost of admission, plan to spend the day.

Lazy, Hazy Days at
TILDEN REGIONAL PARK

Grizzly Peak Blvd. and Canon Dr., Berkeley
(510) 562-7275 (Headquarters)
www.ebparks.org/parks/tilden.htm

Many families visit Tilden Park for its trails, meadows and woods. Others enjoy the park's other delightful activities. Looking for a place to cool off? Head to Lake Anza, a sun-warmed shallow water play area that's open from May to October. Lifeguards are on duty. Spread your blankets, beach chairs and umbrellas on the wide sandy beach. Bring a picnic, or visit the on-site snack bar featuring kid-friendly food and ice cream treats.

The Pony Rides (510-527-0421) are another favorite of park go'ers. Very young children can sit on gentle quarter horses that amble slowly in a circle. Older buckaroos get to ride on horses in a corral. The Little Train (510-548-6100) at the south end of the park offers kids and adults a 15-minute ride on a miniature steam train that goes through a tunnel and around the hillside. Another attraction, the Herschell-Spillman carousel (510-524-6773) boasts beautifully painted wooden animals including colorful frogs and roosters. Adults take note: the carousel's snack bar serves espresso! The Environmental Education Center and The Little Farm round out Tilden Park's other attractions. Read about them on page 135.

SEASONS AND TIMES

➤ Park: Year-round, daily, 5 am—10 pm. Carousel and Little Train: Summer, daily; Sat—Sun in the winter. Pony ride: Summer, daily, 11 am—4 pm; other times, Sat—Sun, 11 am—5 pm. The Environmental Education Center: Year-round, Tue—Sun, 10 am—5 pm. The Little Farm: Year-round, daily, 8:30 am—4 pm.

COST

➤ Park: Free. Carousel: Each ride $1; 13-ride book $10. Little Train: Each ride $1.50; 6-ride book $5. Kids under 2 ride free. Pony ride: 2 and older, $2.50. Be prepared to pay a small fee for Lake Anza.

GETTING THERE

➤ By car, take Hwy. 24 to the Fish Ranch Rd. Exit, just east of the Caldecott Tunnel. Turn north onto Grizzly Peak Blvd. Enter the park at Canon Dr. where Wildcat Canyon Rd. and Grizzly Peak intersect. Free parking on site. About 15 minutes from Hwy. 24.
➤ By public transit, take AC Transit bus 67 from the Berkeley BART station.

NEARBY

➤ U.C. Berkeley campus, Lawrence Hall of Science.

COMMENT

➤ Call each concession or visit the website for up-to-date times and fees. Plan at least a half-day visit.

Fun for all Seasons
YERBA BUENA GARDENS

**Bordered by 4th, Mission, 3rd
and Howard streets, San Francisco
(415) 777-2800
www.zeum.org**

So many fun things to do in one place—it's no wonder families flock to Yerba Buena Gardens. It's a recreational, commercial and arts complex in one. (Read about the artsy offerings at Zeum on page 98.) Young children love the Rooftop Garden, an outdoor play area with a variety of activities for whiling away the afternoon. To reach the Rooftop, walk south on the pedestrian bridge over Howard Street from the main section of Yerba Buena Gardens. Everyone makes a beeline for the colorful antique Looff carousel. It features beautifully restored hand-carved animals. Nearby, the most imaginative Children's Garden and Play Circle has slides, swings and a sandy play area with a stream. The hedge maze is low enough for young children to navigate.

Any bowlers in the family? The main section of the Gardens houses a bowling center with 12 lanes and a café on the second floor. Don your ice skates and take a few turns at the Ice Skating Center. It is San Francisco's only year-round public rink featuring an NHL-sized ice surface. Skate rentals are available.

SEASONS AND TIMES
➤ Rooftop Garden: Call or visit the website for dates and times. Bowling and skating: Call (415) 777-3727.

COST
➤ Free for the gardens, playground, maze and carousel. Fees for bowling and skating.

GETTING THERE
➤ By car, from U.S. 80, take the 5th St. Exit and drive north to Mission St. Park at the 5th and Mission Garage, on Mission between 4th and 5th streets, or the Moscone Garage on 3rd St. between Howard and Folsom streets. About 5 minutes from U.S. 80.

➤ By public transit, take Muni buses 9X, 30 or 45 to Yerba Buena Gardens. Or take the Muni Metro or BART to either the Powell or Montgomery stations.

NEARBY
➤ Museum of Modern Art, Metreon, Zeum, San Francisco Centre, Cartoon Art Museum.

COMMENT
➤ Plan a 2- to 4-hour visit. The café at the Rooftop Garden serves snacks, beverages and meals.

CHAPTER 5

PLACES
TO LEARN

Introduction

Part of the joy of parenting is satisfying your children's endless curiosity about the world around them. There are many places in the Bay Area that will help you do this in a fun way. This chapter features some of the most outstanding learning places. Kids can go on a virtual tour of the universe, produce animated movies, make their own stuffed bear, experience a San Francisco tremor, walk with dinosaurs, peer into the night sky, learn about the Bay's ecology and more. There are many other outstanding places you can visit as well. The resource lists in the "In Your Neighborhood" chapter will help you find the ones in your local community. Just don't tell your kids these outings are educational.

Teddy Bear's Picnic
THE BASIC BROWN BEAR FACTORY

444 DeHaro St., San Francisco
(800) 554-1910
www.basicbrownbear.com

Basic Brown Bear was founded in 1976 and was a traditional factory making children's soft toys. That is until owners realized that children wanted to see how the toy bears were made. They then turned the factory into a safe place where youngsters could visit. They also started the "stuff it yourself" project. Basic Brown Bear provides the pattern, material, stuffing and instructions for making your own bear. Your kids work with staff members to put it together and decide how fat or slender it will be. This usually takes about a half-hour, but the staff is patient with kids who want to spend more time.

The factory has more than 30 bear models (even more outfits) to choose from—so there's one for every taste and budget. The cost of making your own is based on the size and complexity of the pattern. Baby Bear is the least expensive. It stands 13 inches high and costs about a dollar per inch. The factory's free drop-in tours—suitable for families or small groups—reveal the entire bear-building process. Skip the bear-stuffing part of the tour if you dare, but your kids might be grumpy as bears.

SEASONS AND TIMES
➤ Factory: Mon—Sat, 10 am—5 pm; Sun, noon—5 pm. Tours: Sun—Fri, 1 pm; Sat, 11 am and 1 pm.

COST
➤ Visit and tours: Free. Bears: $12 to $999.

GETTING THERE
➤ By car, from I-80 W., take the 9th St./Civic Center Exit and follow the signs for 8th St., continuing until 8th ends at the traffic circle. Turn into the traffic circle and go around it to pick up Henry Adams St. heading south. Adams turns into Kansas St. at Mariposa St. Turn east onto Mariposa and continue 2 blocks to DeHaro St. Red flags mark the factory. Street parking. About 20 minutes from downtown.
➤ By public transit, take Muni bus 19.

COMMENT
➤ Plan a 2-hour visit. Several nearby restaurants offer family-friendly selections of snacks, beverages and meals. Try Sally's (300 DeHaro St., 415-626-6006) for home fries, omelets and baked goods.

A *Love for Learning*
BAY AREA DISCOVERY MUSEUM

Fort Baker, 557 McReynolds Rd., Sausalito
(415) 487-4398
www.badm.org

Families and caregivers, but children especially, enjoy visiting the Bay Area Discovery Museum. And why wouldn't they? The museum occupies six buildings at historic Fort Baker beside the Bay and offers endless hours of exploration and play.

Hands-on exhibits (temporary and permanent) and learning labs are the rule at this museum. The Science Lab, the Art Room and the Media Arts Center have an array of interesting activities for children who enjoy creating—be it with clay, collage, lasers or musical instruments. In the Test Tube building, kids get to try out prototypes of the museum's new exhibits and programs. For example, your children might examine a wood rat's lodge and then try to build one. The Discovery Hall presents changing displays.

The Museum conducts workshops for kids that cover music, movement, ceramics, art and science. There are also special events with entertainment, storytellers and art projects connected to holidays and celebrations.

SEASONS AND TIMES
➺ Summer: Tue—Sun, 10 am—5 pm. Fall: Tue—Thu, 9 am—4 pm; Fri—Sun, 10 am—5 pm.

COST
➺ Individuals $7, under 1 free.

GETTING THERE
➺ By car, from downtown, drive north across the Golden Gate Bridge and take the Alexander Ave. Exit. Follow the signs for East Fort Baker and the Bay Area Discovery Museum. Free parking on site. About 30 minutes from downtown.

NEARBY
➺ Sausalito, Bay Model Visitor Center.

COMMENT
➤ Plan a 2- to 4-hour visit. The Discovery Café has a family-friendly menu.

Explore the Bay
BAY MODEL VISITOR CENTER

**2100 Bridgeway, Sausalito
(415) 332-3871
www.www.baymodel.org**

The Bay Model Visitor Center uses scientific research, public education, interactive workshops and programs to explain San Francisco Bay's natural, cultural and historic aspects to visitors. The highlight is touring the model—not an ordinary display case variety. This one is a scaled replica of the Bay, formed from 15,000 tons of concrete! Maps and an audio tour lead you through it, with signs marking landmarks and waterways from south Bay, to Marin County and the delta.

Until recently this was a working scientific model used to test the impact on the Bay of deepening a shipping channel, developing a shoreline or expanding SF International Airport. Even thought the scientific work is now done on computers, you can still see how the model reproduces the tides, with water flowing in and out under the miniature Golden Gate Bridge just as it does under the real bridge only miles away.

In the paths adjacent to the model are a number of interactive exhibits. Kids can turn knobs, push buttons, watch videos, access a computer or pick up a phone to learn more about the Bay's history and ecology.

An art gallery, a mini-aquarium and a gift shop are under the same roof. There's also a fascinating exhibit on the historic ship building yard that occupied this site during World War II.

SEASONS AND TIMES
➤ Year-round: Tue–Sat, 9 am–4 pm.

COST
➤ Free.

GETTING THERE
➤ By car, take U.S. 101 N. across the Golden Gate Bridge. Take the Sausalito/Marin City Exit onto Bridgeway heading south to Harbor Dr. Turn east on Harbor, then south on Marinship Way and follow the signs to the Bay Model. Free parking on site. About 30 minutes from downtown.
➤ By public transit, take Golden Gate buses 2, 10, 20 or 50 from the Transbay Terminal at Mission and 1st streets in San Francisco. Or take the Sausalito ferry and pick up one of these buses from the Sausalito Ferry Terminal.

NEARBY
➤ Sausalito, Bay Area Discovery Museum.

COMMENT
➤ Bring a picnic. There are tables where you can enjoy lunch and watch the seabirds. Plan a 2-hour visit.

Shaking All Over
CALIFORNIA ACADEMY
OF SCIENCES

Golden Gate Park, San Francisco
(415) 750-7145
www.calacademy.org

"**E**arth, ocean, space, all in one place"—an apt slogan for the home of the Steinhart Aquarium, the Morrison Planetarium and the Natural History Museum.

At the Steinhart Aquarium, awesome reptiles, amphibians and myriad fish species greet you. Kids can stand nose-to-nose with sharks, see alligators, touch tide pool creatures and enjoy a boisterous family of black-footed penguins. The 100,000-gallon Fish Roundabout is alive with hundreds of ocean fish. Daily demonstrations and feedings offer a wealth of information about the animals.

Kids can reach for the stars at the Morrison Planetarium. Some of the displays, such as the meteorites, are hands-on. Take the family for a virtual tour of the universe at one of the sky shows.

The Natural History Museum is one of the top ten natural history museums in the world, and for good reason. One large, walk-through exhibit takes visitors on an exciting journey through 3.5 billion years of Earth's history, complete with sights and sounds from when dinosaurs ruled. Another exhibit features stuffed African animals in their natural habitats.

Hands-on activities throughout the museum give young visitors a better grasp on the natural world. Don't miss the earthquake exhibit. It features a simulated major San Francisco tremor.

SEASONS AND TIMES
➤ Summer (Memorial Day—Labor Day): Daily, 9 am—6 pm (Wed until 8:45 pm). Winter (Labor Day—Memorial Day): Daily, 10 am—5 pm (Wed until 8:45 pm).

COST
➤ Adults $8.50, youths (12 to 17) $5.50, children (4 to 11) $2, under 4 free. Free the first Wednesday of every month. Visitors with a valid Muni bus ticket or transfer receive $2.50 off.

GETTING THERE
➤ By car, from U.S. 101 (Van Ness Ave.), turn west on Pine St. and stay in the 2 left lanes (they merge with Masonic Ave.). Go south on Masonic to Fell St. and turn west. Stay in the 2 right lanes, they become J.F. Kennedy Dr. Continue on JFK. At the third stop sign turn south onto the Music Concourse. The Academy is the large white building. Free parking on site. About 20 minutes from downtown. Note: on Sundays and major holidays, JFK is closed to cars. On Fell St. stay in the 2 left lanes, they merge onto Lincoln Way. Continue west on Lincoln until 9th Ave. and turn north into the park. At the second stop sign turn east onto the Music Concourse.
➤ By public transit, take Muni bus 44 (O'Shaughnessy) to the Academy.

NEARBY
➤ Japanese Tea Garden, Arboretum, Golden Gate Park.

COMMENT
➤ Plan at least a 2- to 4-hour visit.

Out of this World!
CHABOT SPACE & SCIENCE CENTER

10000 Skyline Blvd., Oakland
(510) 336-7300
www.chabotspace.org

Chabot Space & Science Center has interactive exhibits, planetary landscape walk-throughs, meteorites and an amazing array of telescopes, giving visitors a better understanding of space.

What kids like best is touring the universe—thanks to the Center's 3-D technology. They can also visit a full-sized replica of a laboratory on board the International Space Station. Audio and videos will guide them. Another family favorite, the MegaDome Theater, presents stunning films projected onto a 180-degree screen with sound all around. Experience a total solar eclipse, travel to Antarctica or learn what life is like for an astronaut. Other shows in the Planetarium portray the night sky luminous and enchanting. On Friday and Saturday evenings you can do some real star gazing through one of the observatory's powerful telescopes.

SEASONS AND TIMES
➤ Center: Tue—Sat, 10 am—5 pm; Sun, noon—5 pm. Planetarium and Theater: Fri—Sat, 7 pm—9 pm. Telescope viewing: Fri—Sat, 7 pm—10 pm (weather permitting).

COST
➤ Center: Adults $8, youths (4 to 12) $5.50. Planetarium or Theater: Adults $8.75, youths (4 to 12) $6.50. Double Venue (Center, Planetarium or Theater): Adults $14.75, youths (4 to 12) $11. Triple Venue (Center, Planetarium and Theater): Adults $19.75, youths (4 to 12) $15.50. Under 4 free for all events.

GETTING THERE
➤ By car, take I-580 or Hwy. 24 to the Warren Freeway/Hwy. 13 S. Exit. Exit Hwy. 13 at Joaquin Miller/Lincoln Ave. Go east up Joaquin Miller and turn north onto Skyline Blvd. at the traffic lights. Continue on Skyline Blvd. for 1.3 miles. Turn east into the Science Center. On-site pay parking or at the Knoll Lot off Skyline. About 40 minutes from downtown.
➤ By public transit, take BART to the Fruitvale Station in Oakland. Board AC Transit bus 53 and get off at Chabot Space & Science Center.

NEARBY
➤ Jack London Square, USS *Hornet* Museum, Lake Merrit, Children's Fairyland, Oakland Zoo, Oakland Museum.

COMMENT
➤ Plan a 3- to 4-hour visit.

World Class Exploring at
EXPLORATORIUM

**3601 Lyon St., San Francisco
(415) 563-7337 (Information), (415) 561-0362 (Tactile
Dome reservations)
www.exploratorium.edu**

E xploratorium, one of the foremost science museums in the world, is the perfect place for inquiring minds. It features some 650 interactive exhibits designed to teach youngsters about their surroundings. The displays are imaginative—combining science, art, human perception and play to explain light, color, music, language, electricity, sound, weather and more. Kids can clap and make lights blink, stick their hands in a tornado, fly over the Bay (by computer), or blow a bubble larger than their dog.

Want to know why Mom shrunk inside the Distorted Room? Ask one of the Museum's "explainers"—a cadre of high school and college students who interpret the exhibits, and demonstrate holograms, lasers and other intriguing phenomena. The Tactile Dome, one of the most popular attractions, is a cross between a maze and a fun house. Visitors crawl, climb and slide through the pitch-black and experience the most startling textures. There's nothing else like it! The Dome is not recommended for kids under seven, pregnant women or those who are claustrophobic.

SEASONS AND TIMES
➤ Summer: Daily, 10 am—6 pm (Wed until 9:30 pm). Winter: Tue—Sun, 10 am—5 pm (Wed until 9:30 pm). Closed Mondays (except holidays).

COST
➤ Adults $9, youths (6 to 17) $5, children (3 to 5) $2.50, under 3 and members free.

GETTING THERE
➤ By car, take U.S. 101 N. (Van Ness Ave.) to Lombard St. Turn west on Lombard to Lyon St., then go north to Palace Dr. Follow Palace north to the free parking lot. About 20 minutes from downtown.
➤ By public transit, take Muni buses 22, 28, 30, 41, 43, or 45.

NEARBY
➤ Marina, Golden Gate Bridge, Fort Point, Golden Gate
Promenade and Beach.

COMMENT
➤ Plan a 2- to 3-hour visit. Visit the beach and Golden Gate
Promenade across the street with paths for in-line skating, hiking
and biking.

Habitat for Tots
HABITOT CHILDREN'S MUSEUM

**2065 Kitteridge St., Berkeley
(510) 647-1111
www.habitot.org**

A museum for pre-schoolers? Habitot Children's Museum welcomes children as young as infants. This safe and stimulating environment has a wealth of hands-on learning activities, including inviting games that introduce tots to the arts, sciences, history, culture, architecture and technology. Habitot's large space is organized into activity areas. There's an art studio, a "small town" imaginative play area with grocery store and café, and a wind tunnel science lab. The children control the pace and direction of their own learning, choosing whether to play alone or cooperatively. Parents and grandparents can join in the fun.

While the little ones are enjoying themselves, parents and caregivers can browse the resource room for helpful information on parenting and child development. Habitot stages periodic exhibits, workshops and special events to honor the Bay Area's diverse cultural heritage.

The museum is so popular that many families buy a discount booklet of 30 admission passes to cover their weekly visits. This is the perfect place for a toddler's birthday party.

SEASONS AND TIMES
➤ Year-round: Mon and Wed, 9:30 am—1 pm; Tue and Fri, 9:30 am—5 pm; Thu, 9:30 am—7 pm; Sat, 10 am—5 pm; Sun, 11 am—5 pm.

COST
➤ Adults $4, first child (under 7) $6, additional children $3. Adults with infant only $8. Discounts available for seniors and disabled visitors.

GETTING THERE
➤ By car, take I- 80 N. to the University Ave. Exit. Go east on University to Shattuck Ave. and turn south to Kitteridge St. Follow Kitteridge west to the public pay-parking garage in the middle of the block on the south side. About 30 minutes from downtown.
➤ By public transit, take AC Transit buses 65, 67, 7 or 51.

NEARBY
➤ The Hall of Health, U.C. Berkeley campus.

COMMENT
➤ Plan at least a 1- to 2-hour visit.

Body Tips
HALL OF HEALTH

Lower Level, 2230 Shattuck Ave., Berkeley
(510) 549-1564
www.hallofhealth.org

I s there a budding doctor in the house? They'll love Hall of Health. This unique hands-on learning center features a line-up of fun activities and displays about health. While the exhibits are geared for school-aged children, pre-schoolers will enjoy their visit. The museum is co-sponsored by the Children's Hospital in Oakland and Alta Bates Medical Center.

Kids can't wait to handle the medical equipment. They can wear a stethoscope and listen to their hearts beating, look through microscopes, test their reaction times and examine models of human bodies and organs. Electronic quizzes, computer programs and videos on a wide range of health-related topics round out the fun. Friendly and knowledgeable docents will answer questions and demonstrate the displays.

On the third Saturday of each month, families can enjoy the Kids On The Block Puppet Show. These productions explore physical, mental, medical and cultural differences at a kid's level. For a nominal fee (the museum is free), your child can have his or her birthday in a special party room with a presentation.

SEASONS AND TIMES
➤ Year-round: Tue—Sat, 10 am—4 pm.

COST
➤ Free.

GETTING THERE
➤ By car, take I-80 N . to the University Ave. Exit. Go east on University to Shattuck Ave. and turn south to Kitteridge St. Follow Kitteridge west to the public pay-parking garage in the middle of the block on the south side. About 30 minutes from downtown.
➤ By public transit, take AC Transit buses 7, 51, 65, or 67.

NEARBY
➤ Habitot, U.C. Berkeley campus.

COMMENT
➤ Plan a 1- to 2-hour visit.

Fun with Science at
LAWRENCE HALL
OF SCIENCE

**Centennial Dr. (University of California), Berkeley
(510) 642-5132
www.lawrencehallof science.org**

Who says science can't be fun? The Lawrence Hall of Science (LHS) has dozens of hands-on exhibits for 5- to 12-year olds that not only make math, chemistry, biology and astronomy fun, but fascinating as well. Math Rules! is a popular permanent exhibit with a collection of brainteasers. See if your kids don't enjoy honing their problem-solving skills. Just Build It is another kid draw and offers junior engineers the chance to construct houses, bridges—you name it—with large, colorful building blocks. Spectacular special exhibitions, such as the yearly dramatic dinosaur exhibit (they move and roar thanks to robotics) round out the regular displays.

Weekends are special times for families at LHS. There are workshops, such as Chemmystery, where participants solve a make-believe crime using tantalizing clues they test in a lab. The Biology and Computer Labs are open and the Holt Planetarium schedules several shows (recommended for kids over four). On the first and third Saturday of each month, weather permitting, you can view the night sky through astronomical telescopes.

SEASONS AND TIMES
➤ Exhibits: Year-round, daily, 10 am—5 pm. Planetarium: Sat—Sun, 1, 2:15 and 3:30 pm. Telescope viewing: 1st and 3rd Saturday of each month, 8 pm—10 pm, weather permitting.

COST
➤ Adults $7, youths (5 to 18) $5, children (3 to 4) $3, under 3 free.

GETTING THERE
➤ By car, take I-80 E. to the University Ave. Exit. Go east on University to Oxford St., then turn north to Hearst St. Head east on Hearst until Galey Rd. Turn south and follow the signs to Centennial Dr. and LHS. Pay parking lots nearby. About 45 minutes from downtown.
➤ By public transit, use the UC Berkeley Shuttle Service (weekdays only). Board UC's Local Shuttle at Center St. and Shattuck Ave. Transfer to the Hill Service Shuttle at Hearst Mining Circle on campus. Call Transportation Services at (510-643-5708) for information. By AC Transit, take buses 8 or 65 to LHS.

NEARBY
➤ U.C. Berkeley campus, Tilden Regional Park.

COMMENT
➤ Plan a 3- to 4-hour visit.

Get Funky at
ZEUM

**4th and Howard streets, Yerba Buena Gardens,
San Francisco
(415) 777-2800
www.zeum.org**

Zeum is an innovative arts center in downtown San Francisco that offers creative youths and their families an outlet for self-expression. Housed in a huge space, Zeum has studios where up-and-coming artists can experiment using a range of media. One-time drop-in workshops allow participants to create their own animation, produce a multimedia movie, design their own web page and more. There are also amazing weekly classes scheduled just for kids.

Families can work together on projects such as Making Music—a series of brightly-colored masks (actually motion detectors) that trigger sounds and melodies, from cow moans and car horns, to jazz tunes. Kids and adults are invited to play, jump and run around the room and compose their own soundscapes. Not feeling that energetic? Settle back in Zeum's state-of-the-art theater and enjoy a presentation of film, dance or the spoken word.

SEASONS AND TIMES
➤ Summer (Memorial Day—Labor Day): Wed—Fri, noon—6 pm; Sat—Sun, 11 am—5 pm. Open Mon—Fri selected weeks for CampZeum. Winter (Labor Day—Memorial Day): Sat—Sun, 11 am—5 pm. Open Tue—Fri for school field trips, group visits and workshops.

COST
➤ Adults $7, youths (5 to 18) $5.

GETTING THERE
➤ By car, from I-80 W., take the Fremont St. Exit to Howard St. Turn west on Howard. Zeum is located at the southeast corner of Howard and 4th St. Park at the 5th and Mission Garage, on Mission St. between 4th and 5th, or the Moscone Garage on 3rd St. between Howard and Folsom. About 10 minutes from downtown.
➤ By public transit, take Muni buses 9X, 30 or 45 to Yerba Buena Gardens. Or take Muni Metro or BART to either the Powell or Montgomery stations.

NEARBY
➤ Metreon, Museum of Modern Art, Yerba Buena Gardens, Carousel, Rooftop (playground, garden and family-friendly café).

COMMENT
➤ Plan a 2- to 4-hour visit.

CHAPTER 6

MUSIC, THEATER, DANCE AND CINEMA

Introduction

One of the joys of living in a large metropolitan area like San Francisco is enjoying the cultural opportunities it offers. Whether your child wants to hear or play jazz, make a puppet, or attend a mime show, you can find the right place. This chapter has a sampling of the most popular and unusual programs around the Bay Area. There are venues offering families world-class entertainment, and workshops where children can experience the joy of performing, or creating art or music—sometimes under the same roof.

Literally hundreds of community centers, studios and after-school programs in the Bay Area provide children with instruction in music, dance, art and theater. Besides the ones described here, you can find listings in the newspapers—especially the free parenting papers. Always do your research beforehand and ask other families for their recommendations and experiences with particular programs.

All the World's on Stage
CAL PERFORMANCES

**Zellerbach Hall, U.C. Berkeley Campus, Berkeley
(510) 642-9988
www.calperfs.berkeley.edu**

C al Performances offers Bay Area residents what is undoubtedly the most outstanding variety of live performances to be found anywhere. Boasting a lineup of acts that seems to outdo itself each season, the series entertains and thrills audiences with some of the world's best dancers, acrobats, actors, and ethnic and classical musicians. Some of the artists defy categorization.

There are shows for families, too. Each year Cal Performances presents the Family Fare series—three or four performances that are especially appealing to children. The shows in this much-loved series almost always sell out quickly, and for good reason. Parents and children alike delight in the delicious mix and superb quality of the acts, which include puppeteers, dancers and musicians.

SEASONS AND TIMES
➺ Sept—May. Family Fare performances are scheduled throughout the season as weekend matinees. Call the number above or visit the website for exact dates.

COST
➺ Prices for individual seats range from $20 to $50 per show. Series tickets for children under 16 half price. Adult series subscribers receive a 25 percent discount.

GETTING THERE

➤ By car, from I-80 N., take the University Ave. Exit and head east. Turn south onto Oxford and continue on this street until Durant, then turn east. Several University, city and private parking lots are within a few blocks. About 10 minutes from I-80.

➤ By public transit, take BART to Downtown Berkeley Station, or AC Transit buses F, 7, 40, 51, or 64.

NEARBY

➤ U.C. Berkeley campus, Strawberry Canyon Recreation Area, Tilden Park.

COMMENT

➤ For the young at heart, Telegraph Ave. is nearby and offers a colorful street scene with cafés and boutiques to explore before and after the show.

Oakland Does Glamour
PARAMOUNT THEATRE

2025 Broadway, Oakland
(510) 465-6400
www.paramounttheatre.com

An East Bay favorite with lots of family-friendly performances, the Paramount glitters. This wonderfully restored movie palace dating to the 1930s (it's on the National Register of Historic Places) is home to the Oakland Symphony and the Oakland Ballet. Perhaps more interesting to families with young children are the theater's monthly screenings of Hollywood classic films. There are cultural events, too, with presentations that range from jazz and gospel performances, to lively touring entertainers.

Arrive early if you are attending a movie. The theater opens its doors one hour before showtime. That gives you lots of time to wander the spacious lobbies and staircases, and visit the snack bar. Make sure you are seated before the movie starts. You won't want to miss The Mighty Wurlitzer organ, or the historic newsreel, cartoon, previews and give-away game preceding the feature presentation.

SEASONS AND TIMES
➤ Year-round: Call the theater or visit its website for a schedule of upcoming events.

COST
➤ Costs vary depending on the show. To purchase tickets, contact www.ticketmaster.com, or call (415) 421-8497.

GETTING THERE
➤ By car, from Hwy. 580, take Hwy. 980 E. to the 17th St. Exit. Go east on 17th to Telegraph Ave. then north on Telegraph to the theater. The Paramount has parking and several lots are nearby. About 5 minutes from Hwy. 580.
➤ By public transit, take BART to the 19th St. Oakland Station. Or, take AC Transit lines 11, 12, 15, 40, 51 or 59.

NEARBY
➤ Jack London Square, U.C. Berkeley campus.

COMMENT
➤ The building enhances events at the Paramount. Be sure to include time to wander and enjoy the lavish interior.

Tricks of the Trade
PERFORMING ARTS
WORKSHOPS

Most kids jump at the chance to ham it up at least once in a while. Whether your children already have the acting bug or just want to get their feet wet, here are a few great programs to check out.

Young Performers Theatre
Bldg. C, Fort Mason Center, San Francisco
(415) 346-5550
www.ypt.org

The Young Performers Theatre, operating out of Fort Mason, offers kids ages 3 to 15 a variety of dramatic arts classes. Littlest cast members begin with Let's Pretend, an introduction to storytelling, music and puppetry. Those older and more serious about acting can take part in ensemble work and learn audition techniques. Not quite ready for the stage? Take in one of the company's performances. The Young Performer's Theatre mounts eight shows each year with students acting out dramatizations of fairy tales and children's stories. Classes range in price from $150 to $175. Tickets to the shows are $8 for adults and $5 for children.

Julia Morgan Center for the Arts
2640 College Ave., Berkeley
(510) 845-8542
www.juliamorgan.org

The Julia Morgan Center presents an eclectic mix of family-pleasing entertainment—from well-known contemporary and ethnic musicians to stand-up comedy to children's theater. It offers classes, too. Weekly, accomplished performing artists offer youngsters instruction in drama, voice and dance. The Center also features outstanding programs, such as the popular one-day "intergenerational" workshop for children and adults who want to learn about "family clowning" and "hip-hop theater."

Make-A-Circus
755 Frederick St., San Francisco
(415) 242-1414
www.makeacircus.org

Certainly one-of-a-kind, Make-A-Circus is a three-part participatory event. This traveling troupe puts on shows that include a conventional circus with acts and music, workshops in circus skills for families, and lots of audience participation.

In the summer, Make-A-Circus schedules public performances throughout Oakland and San Francisco. It also visits schools and sends specially trained clowns to visit physically and mentally challenged residents of San Francisco Bay Area centers. For information on upcoming shows or to schedule a performance, call the number above or visit the website.

Music on a Grand Scale
SAN FRANCISCO SYMPHONY

Davies Symphony Hall, 201 Van Ness Ave., San Francisco
(415) 864-6000
www.sfsymphony.org

The glory of a full-size live symphony is utterly transporting for some children. If you want to sow the seeds for a love for classical music, then the San Francisco Symphony's Music for Families series is the place to start.

This very popular series features four concerts that are designed to introduce youngsters ages seven and older to the joys of symphonic music. In addition to the music, kids hear an informative talk and see a demonstration of the instruments. Better still, they receive a free activity guide that helps them follow along. The concerts—most are conducted by San Francisco's own much-celebrated Music Director, Michael Tilson Thomas—take place in the early afternoon on Saturdays

Aspiring young musicians might be interested in attending a concert put on by The San Francisco Symphony Youth Orchestra. It features musicians ranging in ages from 12 to 20 who perform three times each season.

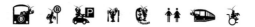

SEASONS AND TIMES
➤ Oct—June: Music for Families takes place on four Saturday afternoons during the Symphony season. Call the number above or visit the website for exact dates.

COST
➤ Music for Families series tickets (4 performances): Adults $46, children (under 12) $23.

GETTING THERE
➤ By car, Davies Symphony Hall is located in the heart of downtown San Francisco. Parking is available in the Performing Arts Garage, 360 Grove St., between Franklin and Gough streets, or in the Civic Center Plaza Garage. Enter it from McAllister between Polk and Larkin.
➤ By public transit, take BART to the Civic Center Station. Or take the Muni Metro (F line) to the Civic Center Station.

NEARBY
➤ San Francisco Public Library, City Hall.

Fresh Air and Tunes
STERN GROVE FESTIVAL

Sigmund Stern Grove, 19th Ave. and Sloat Blvd., San Francisco
(415) 252-6252 (Hotline)
www.sterngrove.org

B illed as San Francisco's "Open House for the Arts," the Stern Grove Festival got its start in 1938 and has been presenting free performances by some of the world's leading musicians ever since. Held on ten consecutive Sundays in the summer, this musical extravaganza offers parents the chance to introduce their families to live performances in a glorious open-air setting.

Go early and enjoy a picnic amidst the giant eucalyptus, redwood and fir trees. Stretch back on your blanket and revel to a crowd-pleasing concert or dance program. The festival features every style—from opera and classical orchestral to avant-garde jazz and world music.

This San Francisco favorite is always packed. Make sure you stake out your place early. Bench and lawn seating are first-come available. Picnic tables can be reserved on the Monday before each concert by calling the San Francisco Recreation and Park Department at (415) 831-5500.

SEASONS AND TIMES
➤ June—Aug: Sun, 2 pm. Call the number above or visit the website for exact dates.

COST
➤ Free.

GETTING THERE
➤ By car, take 19th Ave. south to Sloat Blvd. Turn west on Sloat and continue until Vale Ave. Turn north on Vale into the parking lot. About 5 minutes from 19th Ave.
➤ By public transit, take Muni buses 23 or 28. Or use Muni Metro K or M.

NEARBY
➤ Golden Gate Park, San Francisco Zoo, Ocean Beach.

COMMENT
➤ Come prepared for sun or fog.

Hand-made Creations
VISUAL ARTS WORKSHOPS

C hildren are natural doers. And while looking at art may be fine for a while, soon they're going to want to create their own. Fortunately plenty of places in the Bay Area provide stimulating, creative programs where kids can do just this. Some of the better known, reasonably priced programs are listed below.

Fine Arts Museums of San Francisco

M. H. de Young Museum, 2501 Irving St., San Francisco (temporary location until 2005)
Legion of Honor, near 34th Ave. and Clement St., San Francisco
(415) 863-3330 (24-hour hotline)
or (415) 750-3658 (Family programs)
www.thinker.org/deyoung

The de Young and the Legion of Honor, two of San Francisco's outstanding traditional art museums, are managed by the City of San Francisco. The bulk of the de Young's collection is on loan or in storage until its new facility is completed, but there's still plenty to see and do.

The Family Programs Department has created exciting activities for children at both locations. Doing and Viewing, for 7- to 12-year-olds, features docent-led tours followed by studio workshops. Big Kids/Little Kids leads children three to six years on a walk through the gallery with art classes they can attend with their parents. The department creates special brochures and information for families visiting the museums. Be sure to ask for the kid-oriented guides at the desk near the entrance. You can also call for current schedules and activities. Programs are free after paying the museum entrance fee.

San Francisco Children's Art Center
Building C, Fort Mason Center, San Francisco
(415) 771-0292
www.childrensartcenter.org

Boasting both formal classes and open studios, the Children's Art Center provides children as young as 27 months with an environment for fostering self-awareness, developing self-confidence and exercising their perceptual skills. The classes, which are small and for all ages, explore a wide array of materials and techniques. Kids receive instruction in print-making, sculpture, drawing, painting, collage, puppet making and more.

Regular sessions are held during the school year, but drop-ins are welcome. Art class birthday parties are available.

Sharon Art Studio
Sharon Art Building, Golden Gate Park, San Francisco
(415) 753-7004
www.sharonartstudio.org

Housed in a historic mansion in Golden Gate Park, the Sharon Art Studio (operated by the City of San Francisco Recreation and Park Department) features low-cost classes in drawing, jewelry and ceramics for children under 12. The classes are comprised of 6 to 12 students and led by experienced instructors. On Saturdays, the entire family can enjoy taking a ceramics class together. Special holiday and summer programs are offered.

Studio One
365 – 45th St., Oakland
(510) 597-5027

A little-known treasure, Studio One (run by the City of Oakland Parks and Recreation Department) offers very low-cost after school classes for 6- to 12-year-olds. Kids can try their hand at cartooning, working with clay, jewelry making, mixed media and photography. Studio One offers special holiday programs and summer camps.

Richmond Art Center
2540 Barrett Ave., Civic Center Plaza, Richmond
(510) 620-6772
www.therac.org

This tremendously popular arts facility, operating for over 60 years, is known for its adult programs. But the Center has great activities for kids, too, including weekly afternoon classes (offered year-round), and holiday and summer workshops. Kids as young as three can attend the I Love Art workshops. The sessions feature painting, drawing and sculpture with stories and snacks.

The Center has classes in drawing, painting, crafts and pottery for older children. Experienced teachers oversee the students in well-equipped studios. Classes fill up quickly, so enroll early.

All That's Jazz
YOSHI'S

**510 The Embarcadero W., Oakland
(510) 238-9200
www.yoshis.com**

Yoshi's, the premier jazz club in the Bay Area (perhaps on the West Coast), provides an upbeat and comfortable setting for introducing the younger generation to jazz. Sunday matinees at Yoshi's are affordable times to take the kids to see breathtaking performances by some of the biggest names on the jazz scene—from hard boppers and Latin legends to up-and-coming young musicians.

When members in your brood start to squirm, order them one of Yoshi's luscious desserts. Did someone say "sushi?" Yoshi's excellent adjacent restaurant serves lunch and dinner. Kids will love the floor seating on tatami mats. The club and restaurant are beside Jack London Square, so you can fill out the day strolling along the estuary and visiting the specialty shops.

SEASONS AND TIMES
➤ Year-round: Sunday matinees, 2 pm.

COST
➤ Adults (accompanying children) $10, children $5. General admission from $18 to $24, depending on the performer.

GETTING THERE

→ By car, take Hwy. 880 S. to the Jackson St. Exit. Go west on Jackson to Second St. and turn north. Continue on to Broadway. Go west on Broadway until The Embarcadero where you reach Yoshi's. Validated parking available in adjacent garage. About 5 minutes from Hwy. 880.

→ By public transit, take AC Transit buses A, 58, 59/59A, or 88.

NEARBY

→ Jack London Square, Oakland California Museum.

COMMENT

→ There's no reserved seating, so if you want a booth or a table close to the performers, be there when the doors open.

Yuletide Performances
THE NUTCRACKER

What would Christmas be without an appearance by the Sugar Plum Fairy, the Mouse King or any of the other favorite characters from *The Nutcracker*? This much-anticipated holiday staple with its compelling story, seasonal glitter and bits of magic is a great way to introduce children to dance. Each year, professional and student companies scattered throughout the Bay Area perform *The Nutcracker*. Call the numbers or visit the websites for ticket prices and dates.

San Francisco Ballet
War Memorial Opera House, 301 Van Ness Ave., San Francisco
(415) 865-2000
www.sfballet.org

America's oldest professional ballet company has been performing *The Nutcracker* since 1944 to the delight of parents, children and future dancers. Performances take place in December with extra shows on Christmas Eve and New Year's Eve. Some matinees feature Sugar Plum Parties with holiday music, ballet characters and kids' activities. Call for exact dates and times.

Marin Ballet
Marin Veterans Memorial Auditorium, Marin Civic Center, Avenue of the Flags, San Rafael
(415) 472-3500 (Marin Ballet)
(415) 472-3500 (Ticket Office)

This outstanding community ballet school mounts four *Nutcracker* performances (two matinees and two evening shows on one weekend in December). Dance students star in all but a few of the roles. For an extra fee, families can attend a Candy Cane Party after the matinee performances and mingle with the cast and enjoy snacks.

Oakland Ballet
Paramount Theatre, 2025 Broadway, Oakland
(510) 286-8914
www.oaklandballet.org

This first-rate troupe mounts a highly enjoyable production of *The Nutcracker* with some nice extras.

The All Star Opening Night features guest performances by local celebrities (usually members of the Oakland A's baseball team). For an extra fee, kids can attend a Sweet Dreams party after a matinee to meet cast members and enjoy treats. A special Christmas Eve matinee at 11 am leaves you enough time to decorate the tree or do some last-minute shopping after the performance.

Christmas Revels
Scottish Rite Theater, 1547 Lakeside Dr., Oakland
(510) 893-9853
www.calrevels.org

Christmas Revels is a celebrated tradition for families throughout the Bay Area. Each year the program is reinvented around a Winter Solstice theme from a different part of the globe. Always more than the sum of its parts, the Revels can feature an original or traditional narrative, puppets, song, dance and colorful costumes wrapped together in a refreshing and uplifting show. Performances take place on successive weekends before Christmas.

CHAPTER 7

ANIMALS, FARMS & ZOOS

Introduction

"The world is too much with us," said Wordsworth, suggesting that we look to the natural world for delight. When you've seen enough buildings, people and cars, here are some excursions that are surefire successes for the whole family. At the San Francisco and Oakland zoos, there's no end to the creatures kids can discover. For a close-up look at mammals of the Pacific, head to the Marine Mammal Center and see what conservationists are doing to help save these species. Neighborhood farmers' markets and equestrian stables abound in the area. This chapter provides the names of some of the most accessible ones. You'll learn about the Lindsay Wildlife Museum, too, as well as Tilden Environmental Education Center, Ardenwood Regional Preserve and Lake Merritt Wildlife Refuge.

Some of the sites lie beyond suburban boundaries. For example, if you want to visit a real farm and pick your own produce, you've got to drive a bit. You'll be glad you did.

Farming in the 1800s
ARDENWOOD REGIONAL PRESERVE

34600 Ardenwood Blvd., Fremont
(510) 796-0663
www.ebparks.org/parks/arden.htm

Both a working farm and a living history museum, Ardenwood welcomes visitors to step back in time and experience life at a 19th-century country estate and mansion. You can help the staff perform day-to-day activities, such as planting, tending and harvesting Ardenwood's organic crops. You'll use tools and methods that date back over 100 years. More interesting to younger children are the horse-drawn wagon and train rides that travel around the grounds. The train ride (also powered by horses) recreates the historic railroad that once served Newark and Fremont. It's a favorite with kids. There are blacksmithing and craft demonstrations too, and tours through the Patterson house.

Daily activities at Ardenwood change from season to season. Special events include an old-fashioned Independence Day celebration, summer and fall harvest festivals, music concerts and recreations of Victorian social activities. Fresh-picked organic vegetables are sold just inside the main gate. The stand is open daily from late May through October.

SEASONS AND TIMES
➤ Year-round: Tue—Sun, 10 am—4 pm.

COST
➤ Adults $7, seniors and children (3 to 12) $5. Children under 3 are admitted free, but they must be in strollers, backpacks, carried or held by the hand.

GETTING THERE
➤ By car, from Hwy. 84, take the Ardenwood/Newark Blvd. Exit. Go north on Ardenwood to the entrance of the preserve. Free parking on site. Minutes from Hwy. 84.
➤ By public transit, take AC Transit bus 29 from Union City BART to the bus stop on Newark Blvd. under the freeway. It's a short walk north on Newark.

NEARBY
➤ Paramount Great America, Winchester Mystery House, San Francisco Bay Wildlife Refuge.

COMMENT
➤ Bring sunscreen and hats for everyone. Plan at least a 2-hour visit.

Sitting Tall in the Saddle
EQUESTRIAN STABLES

In this age of amusement parks and video games, many children still get a thrill from horseback riding. Fortunately you don't have to go far in the Bay Area to find stables with horse rentals, riding lessons or guided trail rides. Most of the establishments listed below have horses for riders of every level and offer experienced guides. Some operate day camps where kids can perfect their riding technique and learn about horse care.

Before heading out, call and ask the stable about its operating hours (most are open daily), what equipment it supplies and what you'll need to bring. Helmets are a must, though not every stable provides them. Wear running shoes or riding boots, and long comfortable pants. Bring sunscreen, a water bottle and bug repellent.

Trail rides start at about $30 per person per hour. Prices for lessons vary depending on the length of the session and the level, but expect to pay between $30 and $50 per session.

Here are the names of a few stables within an easy drive of San Francisco.

ANTHONY CHABOT EQUESTRIAN CENTER
14600 Skyline Blvd., Oakland
(510) 569-4428

CHANSLOR RANCH
2660 Coast Hwy. 1, Bodega Bay
(707) 875-3333

CHAPARRAL RANCH
3375 Calaveras Rd., Milpitas
(408) 263-3336

FIVE BROOKS RANCH
8001 State Rte. 1, Olema
(415) 663-1570

GOLDEN GATE PARK STABLES
36th Ave. and JFK Dr., Golden Gate Park, San Francisco
(415) 668-7360

MIWOK LIVERY STABLES
701 Tennessee Valley Rd., Mill Valley
(415) 383-8048

TAYLOR RANCH
5500 Valley View Rd., Richmond
(510) 223-1475

WILDCAT CREEK STABLES
6102 Park Ave., Richmond
(510) 232-6344

To Market to Market
FARMERS' MARKETS

T he same vegetables your kids might reject at the table are often sources of wonderment in the daylight of an open-air farmers' market. There's something about strolling down the aisles and talking to the people who actually grow the fruits and vegetables that adds to the flavor. Kids love this experience. Sometimes you'll find artisans and crafts-makers selling their wares at farmers' markets, and street entertainers performing for the crowds.

Following are just a few of the more popular year-round weekly events that take place around the Bay. There are numerous seasonal farmers' markets, too. In fact, there's hardly a day that you can't find one somewhere.

CIVIC CENTER
Market St. and 7th St., San Francisco
➤ Sun: 7 am—5 pm; Wed, 7 am—5:30 pm.

FERRY PLAZA, SAN FRANCISCO
➤ Tue: 10:30 am—2 pm at the foot of Market St. on The Embarcadero at Justin Herman Plaza. Sat: 8 am—1:30 pm on The Embarcadero at Green St. For information call (415) 353-5650.

MILLBRAE
200 block of Broadway
➤ Sat: 8 am—1 pm.

CIVIC CENTER
Hwy. 101 and San Pedro Rd., San Rafael
➤ Sun and Thu: 8 am—1 pm.

OLD OAKLAND FARMERS MARKET
9th and Broadway, Oakland
➤ Fri: 8 am—2 pm. For information call (510) 745-7100.

DOWNTOWN BERKELEY
Center St. and Martin Luther King
➤ Sat: 10 am—3 pm. For information call (510) 548-3333.

Flocking to
LAKE MERRITT WILDLIFE
REFUGE AND ROTARY
NATURE CENTER

552 Bellevue Ave., Oakland
(510) 238-3739
www.lakemerritt.com

At one time a slough, Lake Merritt is land-locked today—surrounded by the urban landscape. This doesn't seem to bother the waterfowl returning to the lake. Each year more than 50 species of water birds nest around Lake Merritt (it's the oldest wildlife refuge in the United States, created in 1870). Bring your binoculars and field guides. During the course of a year you can see flocks of geese, cormorants, ducks, gulls, herons, egrets, terns and other birds congregating on the five Duck Islands.

Kids can do more than spot birds. The Rotary Nature Center at the water's edge houses nature displays. There are stuffed animals, live tarantulas and other educational exhibits. The working beehive is always a hit! So are the bird feedings that take place daily at 3:30 pm. Nature-based programs are available for schools and other groups.

SEASONS AND TIMES
➤ Year-round: Daily, 9 am–5 pm.

COST
➤ Free.

GETTING THERE
➤ By car, take Hwy. 580 S. to the Grand Ave. Exit. Turn west onto Grand and continue to Bellevue Ave. Go south on Bellevue to Lakeside Park. The Rotary Nature Center is the last city building within Lakeside Park. Free parking on site. About 10 minutes from Hwy. 580.
➤ By public transit, take AC Transit bus 12 or 58.

NEARBY
➤ Children's Fairyland, Jack London Square, Oakland Museum.

COMMENT
➤ Low-key and entertaining for younger kids. Plan at least a 2-hour visit.

The Natural World at Hand
LINDSAY WILDLIFE
MUSEUM

**1931 First Ave., Walnut Creek
(925) 935-1978
www.wildlife-museum.org**

The Lindsay is a unique institution. Part wildlife hospital, museum, and educational center—this conservation organization devotes itself to preserving places for wild animals in the urban environment.

The museum is really an annex to the hospital where thousands of rescued sick and injured creatures, from squirrels to red-tailed hawks, are brought to receive treatment. Animals that can't be returned to the wild live at the museum on display. The Lindsay's educational center features a learning theater and discovery room offering kids lots of hands-on opportunities. But the most popular feature is the Pet Library Program, which enables families to check out rabbits, guinea pigs, hamsters and rats, just as they would borrow a book from the library. It's a great way to see if your kids are ready to take care of their own pet. A Pet Library card is available to members for $5.

There's more. The Lindsay has fascinating classes and workshops on wildlife and conservation that are offered to schools, Scouts, Guides and other groups.

SEASONS AND TIMES

➤ Year-round: Tue—Sun. During the school year, mornings are reserved for school and group tours. Public hours: Tue—Fri, noon—5 pm; Sat—Sun, 10 am—5 pm. Summer hours: Tue—Sun, 10 am—5 pm.

COST

➤ Adults $5, seniors $4, children (3 to 17) $3, under 3 and members free.

GETTING THERE

➤ By car, take Hwy. 24 E. to Walnut Creek. Access 680 N. and take the Treat Blvd./Geary Rd. Exit. Turn east over the freeway and proceed past 2 more lights to Buena Vista. Turn south on Buena Vista to First Ave. and head west. The museum is halfway up the block. Free parking on site. About 10 minutes from Hwy. 24.
➤ By public transit, take County Connection bus 102 from the Walnut Creek BART Station.

NEARBY

➤ John Muir National Historic Site.

COMMENT

➤ Plan a 2-hour visit.

Oceans Alive
THE MARINE MAMMAL CENTER

**Marin Headlands, 1065 Fort Cronkhite, Sausalito
(415) 289-SEAL (7325)
www.tmmc.org**

This animal hospital is dedicated to rescuing and rehabilitating injured and sick marine mammals (seals, sea lions, whales, dolphins and otters). It also offers inspiring public tours that educate all ages about the plight of these creatures. Volunteers explain the general characteristics of marine mammals and the differences between species. Visitors also learn a bit about the treatment the animals receive and the kinds of hazards they encounter in the ocean. About 60 percent of the animals the Center rescues recover and are returned to the wild. Before you come, visit the Center's website. It has pictures of current patients that kids will see during the tour.

This is also a place for learning. The Center conducts nature- and conservation-based programs for schools and groups on-site, at the shore and in the classroom.

SEASONS AND TIMES
➤ Year-round: Daily, 10 am—4 pm. Closed all major holidays.

COST
➤ Free.

GETTING THERE
➤ By car, from Hwy. 101 N., after crossing the Golden Gate Bridge take the first exit off 101 at Alexander Ave. Stay to your right. Proceed about 2 blocks until you see the left turn lane and a sign for "Marin Headlands" (do not go down the hill into Sausalito). Turn west and go through the tunnel. You are now on Bunker Rd. Continue past the stables and cross over Rodeo Lagoon. About halfway alongside the lagoon, the road forks. Bear north up the hill to the parking lot. About 5 minutes from Hwy. 101.

NEARBY
➤ The Marin Headlands—a wonderful natural setting with hiking trails, wildlife watching, Rodeo Beach and historic bunkers.

COMMENT
➤ Plan on spending about an hour at the Center and the rest of the day at the beach, exploring the bunkers and hiking. The Marine Mammal Center maintains an interpretive center at Pier 39 in San Francisco, where a large herd of seals can be viewed from August to June.

Something Wild in the East Bay
OAKLAND ZOO

9777 Golf Links Rd., Oakland
(510) 632-9525
www.oaklandzoo.org

Set in a beautiful location in the Oakland Hills, the Oakland Zoo features over 125 different animal species in biomes that recreate ecosystems in Africa, Asia, Australia and California.

The zoo provides a pleasant atmosphere for a low-key morning or afternoon with smaller children. After looking at the exhibits, visit the children's zoo where kids can pet and feed tame animals. There are rides. For additional fees, you can board a miniature train, a carousel, and a chair lift that offers a panoramic view of the Bay.

The Education Department conducts daylong workshops for students at the zoo that are keyed to the State of California Science Framework. Summer camps are offered for children ages 4 to 12.

SEASONS AND TIMES
➤ Year-round: Daily, 10 am—4 pm. Closed Christmas and Thanksgiving and during inclement weather.

COST
➤ Adults (15 to 60) $6.50, seniors (60 and up) and children (2 to 14) $4.50, under 2 free.

GETTING THERE
➤ By car, take Hwy. 580 S. to 98th Ave. Exit. Turn east on Golf Links Rd. and follow it to the zoo. On-site pay parking ($3). Just a couple of minutes from Hwy. 580.
➤ By public transit, take AC Transit bus 56.

COMMENT
➤ Plan a 2- to 3-hour visit.

Aardvarks to Zebras
SAN FRANCISCO ZOO

Sloat Blvd. and 45th Ave., San Francisco
(415) 753-7080
www.sfzoo.org

A t the San Francisco Zoo, kids come face-to-face with a breathtaking array of exotic and indigenous animals. A long-standing family favorite, the zoo has a strong commitment to wildlife conservation. It houses over 250 species of mammals, birds, reptiles, amphibians, fish and invertebrates in natural settings.

The Children's Zoo, a perennial hit with youngsters, has a barnyard with tame animals—from goats to sheep and donkeys—that kids can pet and feed. Head to the Insect Zoo with its giant millipedes and tarantulas if creepy crawlies are more their thing. The Nature Trail is manned by youth volunteers who are ready to introduce kids to a variety of creatures, including small mammals, birds, reptiles and amphibians.

The narrated Safari Tram tour gives you an overview of these popular attractions and others, including Gorilla World, the meerkat and prairie dog exhibit, the Lion House, the Australian outback station and Penguin Island. Save some time for rides on the Carousel and Little Puffer Steam Train.

Planned activities, such as feeding demonstrations happen daily. The bulletin board near the admissions gate will give you their locations and times.

SEASONS AND TIMES
➤ Year-round: Daily, 10 am—5 pm. Children's Zoo, 11 am—4 pm (summer and weekends, 10:30 am—4:30 pm).

COST
➤ Adults (18 to 64) $9, seniors (65 and up) and youths (12 to 17) $6, children (3 to 11) $3. Discounts for San Francisco residents with ID. General admission includes the Main Zoo, Children's Zoo, Insect Zoo and Barnyard. The rides and tour cost extra.

GETTING THERE
➤ By car, take 19th Ave. to Sloat Blvd. Turn west and continue on Sloat to 45th Ave. Free parking on site. About 30 minutes from downtown.
➤ By public transit, take Muni Metro L, or Muni buses 18 or 23.

NEARBY
➤ Ocean Beach, Cliff House, Lake Merced, Fort Funston.

COMMENT
➤ Wear comfortable shoes—you'll be doing a lot of walking. Be prepared for fog. Plan at least a 4-hour visit.

Going to the Country
SONOMA COUNTY
FARM TRAILS

P.O. Box 6032, Santa Rosa, CA 95406
(707) 571-8288 or (800) 207-9464
E-mail: farmtrails@farmtrails.org
www.farmtrails.org

If you want to pick your own apples, peaches or strawberries, you have to get in your car and drive an hour and a bit out of the city and north to Sonoma County. You can go any time of year and give your kids an opportunity they won't forget. Choose and cut your own Christmas tree, pick a pumpkin for Halloween, pet the cows, buy some goat cheese and visit with the families who live and work on their own farms. Many Bay Area families plan their seasons around these trips. Others have a particular annual trek to a favorite farm where they get to know the proprietors.

Sonoma County Farm Trail maps can be picked up at no charge at any member business and most Chambers of Commerce and Visitor Bureaus in the San Francisco area. You can call, write or e-mail a request for a map. Contact information is given a-bove. Be sure to include your mailing address in your message.

Plan to make a day of your outing and explore the countryside. If you want to pick your own produce at a farm, it's wise to call ahead for hours, prices and information on amenities.

SEASONS AND TIMES
↠ Year-round: Daily.

COST
↠ The day is yours to explore. Pay only for what you buy.

GETTING THERE
↠ By car, take Hwy. 101 N. and follow the directions to the farms of your choice.

Small is Beautiful
TILDEN ENVIRONMENTAL EDUCATION CENTER AND LITTLE FARM

Central Park Dr., Tilden Park, Berkeley
(510) 562-7275
www.ebparks.org/parks/tilden.htm

One of East Bay's most popular parks, Tilden features an Environmental Study Center and Little Farm. Both attractions are immensely popular with local families and visitors whose children like nature and animals.

The Education Center houses a small museum with interactive activities that focus on wildlife and vegetation in the park. A stop here followed by a hike on one of the wooded trails is a great opportunity for everyone to learn about the natural world that begins at the last suburban doorstep.

The Little Farm, with its chickens, pigs, goats, cows and donkey, is a kid favorite. Don't be surprised if your young ones develop a real kinship with the animal residents.

After seeing the animals and displays, go exploring. In addition to hiking trails, the park has a carousel, pony rides, a steam train and a swimming lake (during summer months).

SEASONS AND TIMES
➤ Park: Year-round, daily, 8 am—10 pm. Environmental Education Center: Year-round, Tue—Sun, 10 am—5 pm. The Little Farm: Year-round, daily, 8:30 am—4 pm.

COST
➤ Free.

GETTING THERE
➤ By car, take Hwy. 24 to the Fish Ranch Rd. Exit just east of the Caldecott Tunnel. Turn north onto Grizzly Peak Blvd. Enter the park at Canon Dr. where Wildcat Canyon Rd. and Grizzly Peak intersect. Free parking on site. About 15 minutes from Hwy. 24.
➤ By public transit, take AC Transit bus 67 from the Berkeley BART Station.

COMMENT
➤ You can make a day of it or simply spend an hour visiting the animals and Center.

CHAPTER 8

GREEN SPACES

Introduction

Green spaces abound in the Bay area. Unusual for a region with such a high population, San Francisco has a profusion of federal, regional, district and county parks set aside to preserve the wild natural environment. National Park Service administers two major parks—the 71,000-acre Point Reyes National Seashore and the 76,500-acre Golden Gate National Recreation Area. In them you'll find the Muir Woods National Monument, the historic Presidio and Fort Point, and miles and miles of public beaches.

All of these green spaces were created to protect fragile and irreplaceable ecological communities. But they are more than just a safe haven for plant and animal life. These parks offer Bay Area families and visitors wonderful outdoor experiences. In all but the worst weather, you'll find kids and adults exploring and enjoying the inviting open spaces.

NOTE

Read about other green spaces and preserves in chapters 7 and 9 of this book. And don't forget these popular spots:

Alcatraz (Chapter 1, page 15)

Golden Gate Park (Chapter 1, page 22)

University of California at Berkeley (Chapter 1, page 28)

Island Oasis
ANGEL ISLAND STATE PARK

Ferry departures from Pier 41 (Fisherman's Wharf), San Francisco
(415) 435-1915 (Park), (415) 705-5555 (Ferry)
www.angelisland.com

A ngel Island, situated in the middle of San Francisco Bay, is and the perfect destination for an outing with the family. The fun begins with a 20-minute crossing on the ferry. After disembarking, head for Ayala Cove. It features pretty spots where you can spread out a blanket, or set up base on one of the picnic tables. There is lots of open space for games and tossing a ball.

There's also a lesson or two in history for visitors. Known as the Ellis Island of the West, Angel Island was the point of entry for thousands of Chinese immigrants up until 1940. You can visit the barracks where newcomers were detained. Kids enjoy poking around the old military installations and gun mounts dating from the Civil War. The more adventurous can hike or bike (rentals are available) the mostly level five-mile Perimeter Road that circles the Island. Alternatively, take the one-hour narrated tram tour and see the historic sights and picture postcard views.

SEASONS AND TIMES
➤ Park: Year-round, daily, 8 am—sunset. Ferry: May—Oct, daily;
Nov—April, weekends only. Call for sailing times.

COST
➤ Park: Free. Ferry (round-trip): Adults $11, children (5 to 11) $6,
under 5 free. Tram: Adults $10, children (6 to 12) $7, under 5 free.

GETTING THERE
Board the Blue & Gold ferry from Pier 41.
➤ By car, from The Embarcadero, take North Point St. west to any of
the streets beyond Powell St. Look for parking on the street or in
public pay lots. The parking lots are expensive, and most street
parking is limited to 1 or 2 hours. About 10 minutes from The
Embarcadero.
➤ By public transit, take Muni buses 30, 32 or 42. Or take the Muni
Metro (F line) to Fisherman's Wharf. The Powell-Mason and Powell-
Hyde cable cars have their turnarounds nearby.

COMMENT
➤ Bring your bikes, water bottles, picnic lunch, sporting
equipment and sunscreen. The Cove Café serves deli-style lunches
and also caters picnics. Plan to spend the day.

Hike on the Wild Side
BEAR VALLEY

Point Reyes Park Headquarters, 1 Bear Valley Rd., Olema
(415) 663-1092
www.nps.gov/ggnra

B ear Valley is a magnificent pristine valley
boasting forests and meadowlands. You'll
find it located in the southeastern end of
Point Reyes National Seashore in Marin County.
The Bear Valley Visitor Center (at park headquarters) is the place to begin your discovery of the
area's natural charm. It has interactive habitat
walk-through exhibits that explain about the

creatures living in Bear Valley—including what they eat and where they nest.

Your introduction completed, get ready to explore the park's trails. Rangers help you plan your hike, teach you how to read the maps and talk about safety—don't touch the poison oak! If you have older kids who enjoy hiking, try one of the longer treks such as the trail to Arch Rock and the ocean. The one-mile Earthquake Trail and uphill hike (it's gentle) to Miwok Village (page 184) are easy ones for beginners. Plan to make a day of it and combine Bear Valley with one of the park's wonderful beaches, Heart's Desire, Limantour or Drake's Cove.

SEASONS AND TIMES
➤ Year-round: Daily, sunrise—sunset.

COST
➤ Free.

GETTING THERE
➤ By car, take Hwy. 101 N. to the Central San Rafael Exit and merge onto Irwin St. At 3rd St., turn west (3rd merges into 2nd St., then 4th St., then Red Hill Ave., then Sir Francis Drake Blvd.) Continue west on Drake for 17 miles until it ends at Hwy. 1. Turn north onto Hwy. 1 until Bear Valley Rd. Drive west to the park entrance. Follow the signs to the Visitor Center parking lot. About 1 hour from downtown.

COMMENT
➤ Be sure to carry water bottles, snacks and sunscreen. Stop off at one of the delis in Olema before Bear Valley, and pick up a picnic lunch to have on the trail.

Active Excursions
COASTAL TRAIL

**Golden Gate National Recreation Area (Baker Beach to Fort Funston), San Francisco
(415) 561-3000 (Information) or
(415) 556-8642 (Cliff House Visitor Center)
www.nps.gov/goga**

For dramatic vistas of the rugged California coast, hit the Coastal Trail. You can access the trail almost anywhere (from Fort Funston in the south to Baker Beach in the north). A good place to begin is the Sutro Heights Park section just north of Cliff House. Here you'll see the ruins of the Sutro Baths—once the largest indoor swimming pool in the world with a capacity of 20,000. You can also observe colonies of seals basking on Seal Rock and albatrosses diving for their fish dinner.

Following the path north and through a tunnel brings you to a fenced ledge with an awesome view of the thundering surf below. (Keep an eye on the youngsters in your group.) To explore the charming trails along the cliffs, retrace your steps through the tunnel and climb the hill. These trails lead north through Lincoln Park and on to Baker Beach (page 158). Along the way (after Lincoln Park) you'll pass through some of San Francisco's most stylish neighborhoods.

Don't expect to see the whole trail your first time out—it stretches for miles. Choose a section you want to explore and look for parking nearby. Bikes, in-line skates and roller skates are permitted on many stretches. Telephones, restrooms and picnic tables are located at the beaches and other sites along the trail.

SEASONS AND TIMES
➤ Year-round: Daily, 6 am–10 pm.

COST
➤ Free.

GETTING THERE
➤ By car, take U.S. 101 (Van Ness Ave.) to Geary St. Head west on Geary to Pt. Lobos Ave. Veer northwest to Sutro Heights Park. Free parking on site. About 20 minutes from downtown.
➤ By public transit, take Muni buses 18 or 38AX to Sutro Heights Park.

NEARBY
➤ Ocean Beach, China Beach, Cliff House, Baker Beach.

COMMENT
➤ Take water bottles, sunscreen and snacks. Plan a 2- to 3-hour visit.

Gone Fishin'
LAKE MERCED

**Bounded by Sloat, Skyline, Lake Merced and Sunset boulevards, San Francisco
(415) 831-2700 (SF Parks and Recreation Department)
http://www.parks.sfgov.org**

Trout fishing? In San Francisco? Lake Merced Park, with more than 700-acres, offers families more than just fishing. This recreational haven also has boating, windsurfing, picnicking, bicycling and other pleasant outdoor activities. Bird watching is on the menu as well. The lake's seven miles of shoreline support rushes where migratory birds stop to rest. The isthmus in the lake supports a municipal golf course, and Harding Park with its forest of eucalyptus, cypress and pine trees.

You can rent rowboats, paddleboats, canoes and kayaks and explore the lake. Feel like dipping a line? Fishing rods are available. For the best action, row to the north and west shores. These sections are stocked with trout and you'll most likely catch a fish or two. If sailing interests your kids, sign them up for lessons at the Lake Merced Boating and Fishing Company.

Lake Merced is an emergency reservoir for the city—swimming and gas-powered motorboats are not permitted.

SEASONS AND TIMES
➤ Park: Year-round, daily. Boat rental: Year-round, daily, 6:30 am—sunset.

COST
➤ Park: Free. Boat rental and sailing lessons: Call (415) 681-3310 for information.

GETTING THERE
➤ By car, take 19th Ave. south to Sloat Blvd. and turn west onto Sloat. Continue until Skyline Blvd. and turn south. Skyline brings you to the lake. Free parking on site. About 20 minutes from downtown.
➤ By public transit, take Muni buses 18 or 88 to Lake Merced.

NEARBY
➤ Ocean Beach, Cliff House, Golden Gate Park.

COMMENT
→ The Boathouse Restaurant (1 Harding Park Rd.; 415-681-2727)
serves family fare and the boat rental sells snacks. Or bring a lunch
as picnic tables dot the lakeside. Plan a 2- to 3-hour visit.

Urban Unwinding at
MOUNT TAMALPAIS
STATE PARK

801 Panoramic Hwy., Mill Valley
(415) 388-2070 or (800) 444-7275 (camping reservations)
www.parks.ca.gov

Mount Tamalpais rises to a dramatic 2,500 feet and dominates the landscape of the San Francisco Bay Area. A popular spot for hiking and mountain biking, Mount Tam as it's fondly called, has some 200 miles of trails that meander through redwood groves and beside fern-banked waterfalls. The higher-elevation trails provide some of the world's most breathtaking views—from San Francisco and the Golden Gate Bridge to the Pacific Ocean and the rolling hills of Marin County.

A fun and easy hike for families is the short Verna Dunshee Trail that loops around Mount Tam's highest peak. For a longer hike, try the Matt Davis Trail. It cuts across the mountain for almost seven miles toward Stinson Beach.

Mountain biking is permitted on fire and paved roads in the park. Interested in staying overnight? Mount Tam has two campgrounds located at Pantoll and Steep Ravine. Pantoll features 16 walk-in tent sites, available first-come, first-served (at the Pantoll Ranger Station). Reservations and parking permits are required for the Steep Ravine site on the bluffs near Stinson Beach.

SEASONS AND TIMES
→ Year-round: Daily. Camping permits required for overnight stays.

COST
→ Park: Free. Call camping reservation line above for fees.

GETTING THERE
→ By car, take Hwy. 101 N. to the Mill Valley/Rte. 1 Exit. Go west through Mill Valley and follow the signs to Rte. 1, Stinson Beach and Mount Tamalpais. Free parking on site. About 30 minutes from downtown.

NEARBY
→ Muir Woods.

COMMENT
→ Rock Spring, Laurel Dell Meadow and East Peak Summit have picnic tables. East Peak also has a snack bar. Mountain Home Inn (415-381-9000) serves breakfast on weekends, and lunch and dinner Tuesday through Sunday. Bring your bikes, water bottles, a picnic and sunscreen. Plan to spend the day.

San Francisco's Roots
MOUNTAIN LAKE PARK

Lake St. (Funston Ave. to 8th Ave.), San Francisco
(415) 831-2700
http://parks.sfgov.org

his is the site where in 1776, Spanish soldiers led by Juan Bautista de Anza camped and "discovered" what is now considered San Francisco. Mountain Lake Park is a relatively secluded area, but spacious. There are trails for hiking and bike riding and grassy fields where you can throw a ball or play games. Ask your kids if they can find the rock bearing a plaque that commemorates the arrival of Juan Bautista de Anza and his men.

Perhaps the biggest attraction is the lovely four-acre Mountain Lake. It supplied the city with its drinking water during the Gold Rush. Today ducks, swans, frogs and other water-loving creatures use the lake. The shoreline is framed with lofty reeds and willows and offers lots of interesting spots where up-and-coming naturalists can poke around. Spread a blanket at the tiny beach. It's a pretty setting for lunching and taking in the splendor.

SEASONS AND TIMES
➤ Year-round: Daily, 6 am—9 pm.

COST
➤ Free.

GETTING THERE
➤ By car, take U.S. 101 (Van Ness Ave.) to Geary St. Head west on Geary to 8th Ave. and turn north to Mountain Lake Park. Free parking on site. About 15 to 20 minutes from downtown.
➤ By public transit, take Muni buses 44, 28 or 28L to the park.

NEARBY
➤ The Presidio, Fort Point, Palace of Legion of Honor.

COMMENT
➤ In addition to the beach, the park has tables and lots of grassy areas where you can picnic. Plan a 2- to 3-hour visit.

Towering Trees at
MUIR WOODS NATIONAL MONUMENT

Muir Woods Rd., Mill Valley
(415) 388-2595 (Recorded information)
or (415) 388-2596 (Rangers)
www.nps.gov/muwo

Muir Woods is where you find the world's most famous stand of old-growth redwoods. Many of these behemoths reach 250 feet and were growing during the Crusades. Little wonder tourists from all over the world visit Muir Woods. The overflow parking lot and main trails are often full by noon. Still, the majesty of the place casts a calm on the activity.

You can wander the six miles of trails on the canyon floor and gaze up at the trees. Many of the trails are smooth and level, accommodating wheelchairs and strollers. With little kids, make short loops around the groves using the four bridges spanning Redwood Creek. The tallest trees are along the Main Trail in Bohemian Grove (a half-mile loop) and Cathedral Grove (a one-mile loop). If you head up the canyon on the unpaved trails you'll soon leave the throngs of tourists behind and enter the stillness of the forest. Bring jackets or sweatshirts since the redwood groves are often cool and foggy. Caution: stay on the trails to avoid poison oak and stinging nettles.

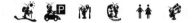

SEASONS AND TIMES
➤ Park: Year-round, daily, 8 am—sunset. Visitor Center: Year-round, daily, 9 am—4:30 pm.

COST
➤ Adults $2, children up to 17 are free.

GETTING THERE
➤ By car, take Hwy. 101 N. to the Mill Valley/Rte. 1 Exit. Go west through Mill Valley and continue west to Rte.1 and Panoramic Hwy. Follow the signs to Muir Woods National Monument—it is well marked. Free parking on site. About 30 minutes from downtown.

NEARBY
➤ Mount Tamalpais State Park.

COMMENT
➤ Picnics are not allowed in Muir Woods. The snack bar near the Visitor Center serves family-friendly food. Plan a 2-hour visit.

Big Tree Country
REDWOOD REGIONAL PARK

**Joaquin Miller at Redwood Rd., Oakland
(510) 562-7275 (Information) or
(510) 482-0971 (Roberts Recreation Area)
www.ebparks.org**

This huge park high in the Oakland Hills is home to a forest of Pacific Coast redwoods—spectacular towering trees that grow more than 100 feet tall. Before ship-to-shore radio and radar, sea captains sailing into San Francisco Bay used the tallest trees on the crest of these hills as a landmark. They could see them from as far as 16 miles out at sea!

Throughout the forest there are trails for hiking, biking and even riding horses, that give you a closer look at the redwoods. Along the trails, you'll discover streams and creeks to explore and picnic areas with barbecues. The park boasts a playground and Roberts Recreation Area. It features a public pool with snack bar and change rooms, an archery range and amphitheater with a fire circle. The latest and most magnificent addition to the park is the Chabot Space & Science Center (page 90).

SEASONS AND TIMES
➤ Park: Daily, 5 am—10 pm. Roberts Recreation Area: Call for times.

COST
➤ Free. Fee for the pool and certain other activities.

GETTING THERE
➤ By car, take I-580 or Hwy. 24 to the Warren Freeway/Hwy. 13 S. Exit Hwy. 13 S. at Joaquin Miller/Lincoln Ave. Go east on Joaquin Miller and turn north onto Skyline Blvd. and the park entrance. Free parking on site. About 40 minutes from downtown.
➤ By public transit, take BART to the Fruitvale Station in Oakland. Transfer to AC Transit bus 46 or 53 and ride it to the park.

NEARBY
➤ Jack London Square, USS *Hornet* Museum, Lake Merritt, Children's Fairyland, Oakland Zoo, Oakland Museum, Chabot Space & Science Center.

COMMENT
➤ Plan a 3- to 4-hour visit.

Camping and Canyons at
SAMUEL P. TAYLOR
STATE PARK

Off Sir Frances Drake Blvd., Lagunitas
(415) 488-9897 or (800) 444-7275 (camping reservations)
www.parks.ca.gov

During the Gold Rush, Samuel P. Taylor and some friends sailed an old schooner from Boston to California. Taylor made a small fortune mining gold and purchased 100 acres of timberland—the present State Park. He established a resort hotel and opened Camp Taylor, one of the first outdoor recreational camping sites.

Today the park invites visitors to explore trails that wind through canyons with fern-filled groves and majestic coast redwoods. Or investigate the grassland section of the park where oaks and madrones offer shade. Hike to the top of Mount Barnabe (the trails are easy) and watch hawks and other large raptors soar over the countryside. In season, Pacific salmon migrate up Papermill Creek to spawn. Kids never tire of watching the fish make their dramatic ascent past the creek's waterfalls and rapids.

Bring your bikes. There is a three-mile paved scenic trail that is gentle and level; perfect for young bicyclists. The park has picnic areas and 60 campsites—each with a picnic table, wood stove, food locker and parking space. Bathrooms and hot showers are nearby.

SEASONS AND TIMES
➤ Year-round: Daily, sunrise—sunset. Camping permits required for overnight stays.

COST
➤ Park entrance fee: $2 per car (includes parking). Camping: $12 per campsite

GETTING THERE
➤ By car, take Hwy. 101 N. to the Central San Rafael Exit and merge onto Irwin St. At 3rd St., turn west (3rd merges into 2nd St., then 4th St., then Red Hill Ave., then Sir Francis Drake Blvd.). Continue west on Drake until you reach the park entrance with its office and visitor center. The parking is free along Sir Francis Drake, but cars sometimes speed along this narrow road. It's much safer to pay the small entrance fee and park inside. About 40 minutes from downtown.

COMMENT
➤ Bring your bikes, water bottles, picnic and sunscreen. Plan to
spend the day.

A *Real Jewel!*
TILDEN REGIONAL PARK

Grizzly Peak Blvd. and Canon Dr., Berkeley
(510) 562-7275 (Headquarters)
www.ebparks.org/parks/tilden.htm

Tilden Park really does have something for everyone. Young kids enjoy visiting the Nature Area with its Little Farm and cuddly animals. Older children like the interactive displays at the Environmental Education Center. It has easy-to-use microscopes for viewing pond life, a fascinating "underground" journey through a watershed and more.

Interested in exploring the park's trails? The Center has maps for self-guided nature hikes. All of the trails, ranging from a half-mile to several miles, are clearly marked and within easy reach of restrooms. A standout for families is the boardwalk hike through a marsh to Jewel Lake. At the lake, kids can look for turtles snoozing on logs. Depending on the time of the visit, they might also see a brood of fuzzy baby ducks lined up and paddling after their mother.

On weekends, the Environmental Education Center has special planned activities for families. Pick up a schedule at the Center, or check the local newspaper for upcoming events. Read about

Tilden Park's other attractions for families on pages 77 and 135 in this guide.

SEASONS AND TIMES

➤ Park: Year-round, daily, 5 am—10 pm. Environmental Education Center: Year-round, Tue—Sun, 10 am—5 pm. Little Farm: Year-round, daily, 8:30 am—4 pm.

COST

➤ Free.

GETTING THERE

➤ By car, take Hwy. 24 to the Fish Ranch Rd. Exit just east of Caldecott Tunnel. Turn north at Grizzly Peak Blvd. Enter the park at Canon Dr. where Wildcat Canyon Rd. and Grizzly Peak Blvd. intersect. Free parking on site. About 15 minutes from Hwy. 24.

➤ By public transit, take AC Transit bus 67 from Berkeley BART Station.

NEARBY

➤ U.C. Berkeley campus, Lawrence Hall of Science.

COMMENT

➤ Bring sunscreen, water bottles and comfortable clothes that cover your arms and legs if hiking. Plan at least a half-day visit.

CHAPTER 9

THE BAY, BEACHES AND ECOLOGY PRESERVES

Introduction

With all their unique qualities, it's probably the Bay itself and the Pacific Ocean that makes San Francisco and the Bay Area the special place it is. Not only does the incredible landscape contribute to the natural beauty of the surroundings, it also provides families with loads of wonderful activities. Though swimming is possible in a few select spots, beware, the water is awfully cold. Still, the Bay and ocean beaches are great places to run, hike, bike, in-line skate, picnic, fly kites, explore sand dunes, observe wildlife and fish. For fresh air, creative play, relaxation and just plain fun, it's hard to do better than a day at the beach.

Take the Plunge
AQUATIC PARK

Hyde and Jefferson streets, San Francisco
(415) 556-0560 (National Park Service)
www.nps.gov/safr

This small swimming beach located near Hyde Street Pier and Ghirardelli Square (page 18) is a favorite play spot for the younger set. The water is cold, but kids don't mind, especially on warm days. In fact even when foggy, children want to kick off their shoes and socks, roll up their pants and wade right in. Hardy San Franciscans swim regularly at Aquatic Park. It's also popular with canoeists and kayakers because the water is always calm. Bring pails and shovels. The sand is perfect for building sculptures. Depending when you visit, you might witness Aquatic Park's sandcastle contest.

On most days, street musicians or drummers are nearby, creating a festive atmosphere. Save time to visit the quiet harbor that surrounds the beach. Flanked with sailboats and small fishing boats, the harbor is also home to the world's largest fleet of historic ships moored at the adjacent Hyde Street Pier.

SEASONS AND TIMES
➤ Year-round: Daily, dawn—dusk.

COST
➤ Free.

GETTING THERE
➤ By car, take The Embarcadero north to North Point St. Turn west on North Point and continue for about 9 blocks to Ghirardelli Square Garage, or look for street parking. About 15 minutes from downtown.
➤ By public transit, take Muni bus 19, or the Hyde St. cable car.

NEARBY
➤ Ghirardelli Square, National Maritime Museum, Hyde St. Pier, The Cannery.

COMMENT
➤ Make sure everyone has a towel and change of clothes in their daypack.

Look What's Cooking
BAKER BEACH

**Gibson Rd., San Francisco
(415) 556-8371
www.nps.gov/goga**

H ere's the perfect place where your kids can run to their heart's content. The water at Baker Beach has a strong rip tide and is unsafe even for wading, but the long expanse of fine sand is ideal for building castles, tossing a ball, flying kites, exploring dunes or enjoying a picnic barbecue. The barbecues are supplied.

The beach boasts million-dollar views of nearby Golden Gate Bridge with ships passing by, the rugged Marin Headlands directly across the strait, and the occasional pelican or seal bobbing in the water. For active kids, Baker Beach is a great outdoor play area even when the weather is cool. During one of San Francisco's warmer days, it's *the* place to be.

SEASONS AND TIMES
→ Year-round: Daily, dawn—dusk.

COST
→ Free.

GETTING THERE
→ By car, from downtown, take California St., Geary Blvd. or Fulton St. west to 25th Ave. Turn north to Lincoln Blvd. Follow Lincoln first east and then north to Gibson Rd. Turn west to the beach. Free parking on site. About 20 minutes from downtown.
→ By public transit, take Muni bus 29.

NEARBY
→ Golden Gate Bridge, Fort Point, Presidio.

COMMENT
→ It can be windy so bring jackets or sweatshirts.

A *Hidden Gem*
CHINA BEACH

**Sea Cliff Ave., San Francisco
(415) 556-8371
www.nps.gov/goga**

A delightful day is in store for families who are willing to look for this secluded little beach. Hidden below the stunning homes in the Seacliff area, China Beach features a protected 600-foot stretch of sand tucked between two cliffs. This is one of the few beaches in San Francisco that is partially sheltered from the treacherous waves. The water is usually gentle enough for wading, but it is chilly and there are no lifeguards—swimming is not advised.

At low tide, you can explore the tide pools. Be careful not to trample the tide pool creatures and don't move them away from their homes. Not in the mood for sand? Then stretch out on your beach towel on the enclosed sundeck. Like those living in the palatial mansions on the cliffs above, you can enjoy incredible views of the Golden Gate Bridge and the Marin Headlands.

SEASONS AND TIMES
➤ Year-round: Daily, dawn—dusk.

COST
➤ Free.

GETTING THERE
➤ By car, from downtown, take California St., Geary Blvd. or Fulton St. west to 25th Ave. Turn north to Del Mar. Turn 1 block west to 26th Ave. then north to Sea Cliff Ave. There's a pay lot or street parking. About 20 minutes from downtown.
➤ By public transit, take Muni bus 1 (California St.); it stops a few blocks from the beach.

NEARBY
➤ Golden Gate Park, Cliff House, Baker Beach, Palace of the Legion of Honor, Presidio.

COMMENT
➤ Take strollers down to the beach using the ramp on the left. Have jackets handy if a fog rolls in. Some maps label this area James D. Phelan Beach State Park.

Beaches, Boats and Barbecues
COYOTE POINT COUNTY RECREATIONAL AREA

**Off U.S. Hwy. 101 S., San Mateo
(650) 573-2592
www.coyoteptmuseum.org**

This 670-acre park has it all. There's a swimming beach on the Bay, grassy playing fields and playgrounds, walking and biking trails, barbecue and picnic area, fishing jetty, boat ramp and a wheelchair ramp. For most kids just being on the beach can be exciting, since daring windsurfers dart close by and overhead planes make dramatic final approaches to the airport.

Don't forget to check out Coyote Point Museum (1651 Coyote Point Dr.; 650-342-7755). This nationally recognized institution has four levels of interactive exhibits on the environment and the Bay. Check out the aquarium and Wildlife Habitat Exhibit featuring 25 native animals in indoor and outdoor displays. The museum puts on interesting activities for children, where they can meet some of the animals face-to-face. In addition to a well-stocked nature store, the museum has gardens that attract hummingbirds and butterflies. The charming picnic area can be reserved.

SEASONS AND TIMES
➤ Park: Year-round, daily, dawn—dusk. Museum: Year-round, Tue—Sat, 10 am—5 pm; Sun, noon—5 pm.

COST
➤ Recreation Area: $4 per car. Museum: Adults $3, youths (13 to 17) $2, children (4 to 13) $1. Free first Wednesday of every month.

GETTING THERE
➤ By car, take U.S. 101 S. to San Mateo and look for signs to the County Recreation Area. Free parking on site. About 20 minutes from downtown.

NEARBY
➤ Hiller Museum of Aviation, San Francisco International Airport.

COMMENT
➤ Bring your own snacks and drinks, or a picnic. There is no restaurant.

Step into
CRAB COVE

1252 McKay Ave., Alameda (Visitor Center)
(510) 521-6887
www.ebparks.org/parks/crab.htm

Most parks dotting the East Bay shoreline allow you to access the Bay and its wonderful wildlife, but none is as popular as Crab Cove and the Alameda Shoreline. And no wonder. It features several miles of sandy beaches with calm water where kids can swim and play.

The first estuarine reserve of its kind in California, Crab Cove offers visitors the chance to wade into the water and study the plants and animals living there. An hour in the reserve is a wonderful environmental lesson in caring for the natural riches of the Bay.

There's more. The Visitor Center has exciting three-dimensional exhibits explaining the Bay's ecosystem. You won't need SCUBA gear to see what's happening. The Center's large saltwater aquarium is alive with native creatures. Staff naturalists are on hand to lead families in educational programs, nature walks and demonstrations. Don't forget to visit the Elsie B. Roemer Bird Sanctuary (Shoreline Dr. and Park Ave.) at the southern end of the beach. It has a saltwater marsh where myriad shorebirds and waterfowl can be observed.

SEASONS AND TIMES
➺ Bird sanctuary and reserve: Year-round, daily, dawn—dusk.
Visitor center: Mar—Dec, Wed—Sun, 10 am—4:30 pm.

COST
➺ Free.

GETTING THERE
➺ By car, from Hwy. 880, take the Alameda/Webster St. Tube Exit and go west on Webster St. to Central. Drive north to McKay and Shoreline Dr. Free parking on site. About 20 minutes from the 880.
➺ By public transit, take AC Transit buses 50 or 63.

NEARBY
➺ Oakland Museum, USS *Hornet* Museum, Lake Merritt, Children's Fairyland.

COMMENT
➺ Bring snacks and drinks or pack a picnic to enjoy on the beach. Remember the sunscreen and toys.

Hanging Out
with the Hang-gliders
FORT FUNSTON

Off the Great Hwy., San Francisco
(415) 556-8642 or (415) 556-8371
www.nps.gov/goga

Step back in time at Fort Funston. It features the original, windswept sand dunes that dominated much of San Francisco's ocean coastline until the Gold Rush. For many years this was a military lookout and base. The abandoned gun emplacements held 150-ton guns during World War II and are still visible, while the parking lot was a missile site during the Cold War.

Today, Fort Funston is a popular spot for hang-gliders. Take the kids on a hike down to the beach, or watch from the viewing platform as these daredevils take off from the cliffs and soar on the ocean breeze. A one-mile paved loop, called Sunset Trail, is a perfect spot to watch the sun dip below the Pacific Ocean. It connects with the Coastal Trail (page 142), which leads north to Ocean Beach (page 168). Don't feel that adventurous? Check out the greenhouse near the Visitor Center to see the native plants that park rangers are re-introducing to the dunes with the help of school children and volunteers.

A few cautions will ensure your visit is safe: stay on the marked trails as some of the roads go nowhere— they were designed to confuse the enemy in wartime; and keep children away from cliff edges and the water (dangerous rip tides exist).

SEASONS AND TIMES
➤ Year-round: Daily, 6 am—10 pm. Visitor Center: Sat—Sun, noon—4 pm.

COST
➤ Free.

GETTING THERE
➤ By car, from downtown, take Geary Blvd. west. It becomes Point Lobos Ave. then the Great Hwy. as you follow the road south at Cliff House. Or, take Market St. southwest (it becomes Portola Dr.) to Sloat Blvd. and drive west to the Great Hwy. Go south on the Great Hwy. to Skyline Blvd. or John Muir Dr. Watch for signs to Fort Funston. Free parking on site. About 30 minutes from downtown.
➤ By public transit, take Muni buses 18 or 88.

NEARBY
➤ San Francisco Zoo, Ocean Beach, Lake Merced.

COMMENT
➤ Bring jackets if foggy or windy.

Calling all Bikers and Hikers
GOLDEN GATE PROMENADE

Golden Gate National Recreation Area, San Francisco
(415) 556-0560 (National Park Service)
www.nps.gov/goga

Pack your bike, in-line skates, snacks and water bottles and set off to enjoy three-and-a-half miles of gorgeous Bay shore trail.

Begin your excursion at Fort Point near the Golden Gate Bridge, taking the Promenade east toward Marina Green. You can stop anywhere along the way and see skilled and daring windsurfers on the water.

Make sure you visit Crissy Field. It features newly restored dunes and a wetland ecology preserve kids can explore. Take another breather further on at Marina Green, where everyone can ogle the two-handed stunt kites. Be sure to check out the Wave Organ, a walk-in stone sound sculpture east of the Marina Green jetty. The fractured columns and granite amphitheater are arranged around pipes that "play" the waves with low moans and backwash gurglings. Even if the Wave Organ doesn't play, your kids will enjoy watching the endless parade of pleasure craft and huge ocean-going ships.

SEASONS AND TIMES
→ Year-round: Daily, dawn—dusk.

COST
→ Free.

GETTING THERE
→ By car, from downtown, take Marina Blvd. west to Marine Dr. and follow the signs to Fort Point. Park in any of the many free lots. About 20 minutes from downtown.
→ By public transit, take Muni buses 22, 28 or 29.

NEARBY
→ Golden Gate Bridge, Presidio, Exploratorium, Ghirardelli Square, Aquatic Park, National Maritime Museum, Hyde St. Pier.

COMMENT
→ It can be windy along the Promenade so bring jackets or sweatshirts.

Walk into a Picture Postcard
MARIN HEADLANDS

Fort Barry, Building 94B, Marin (Visitor Center)
(415) 331-1540 or (415) 556-0560 (Recreation Area)
www.nps.gov/goga/

The Golden Gate National Recreation Area spans the Golden Gate and includes the Marin Headlands. The headlands, which cover a vast area, comprise rolling hills, bunkers and fortifications, a beach and lagoon, a marine mammal rehabilitation center and the rugged Pacific coast shores.

After you cross the bridge, stop at Vista Point to take in the famous panoramas of the San Francisco skyline framed in the bridge's golden-orange towers. As you move into the headlands, you'll find about a 100 miles of paved roads; unpaved fire roads; foot, mountain bike, and horse trails to explore.

If you only have time for a short visit, drive along scenic Conzelman Road, the headlands' main access that hugs the cliffs to Point Bonita. Once there, a half-mile hike takes you to the 1855 Point Bonita Lighthouse perched high on the rocky cliffs. It offers a breathtaking view of the bridge and San Francisco beyond. Explore the nearby old military fortifications, tunnels and bunkers, some dating back to the 1870s. Or, make your way to Rodeo Beach with its tide pools filled with sea anemones and starfish, and surfers who ride the waves. The beach is unsafe for swimming, though you can wade in the water. Pelicans, loons and other water birds populate the lagoon next to the beach.

SEASONS AND TIMES
➤ Rodeo Beach and lagoon: Year-round, daily, dawn—dusk. Visitor Center: Year-round, daily, 9:30 am—4:30 pm. Lighthouse: Year-round, Sat—Mon, 12:30—3:30 pm.

COST
➤ Free.

GETTING THERE
➤ By car, take U.S., 101 N. across the Golden Gate Bridge. Get off 101 at the Sausalito Exit and access Conzelman Rd. Free parking on site. About 30 minutes from downtown.
➤ By public transit, take Muni bus 76 (it operates Sundays only).

NEARBY
➤ Marine Mammal Center, Bay Area Discovery Museum, Sausalito, Bay Model, Muir Woods, Mount Tamalpais State Park.

COMMENT
➤ Bring long pants, sweatshirts and flashlights to explore the bunkers, cameras for the postcard views, and towels and toys for the beach. There is no food service on the headlands.

Surf's up at OCEAN BEACH

The Great Hwy. between Cliff House and Sloat Blvd., San Francisco
(415) 556-8642 or (415) 556-8371
www.nps.gov/goga/

Kids, Frisbees™, kites, dogs, bikers, 'bladers, strollers, beach balls and picnickers—all share San Francisco's most popular beach. Ocean Beach, on the Pacific Ocean side of the city, is a flat, four-mile stretch of sand edged with a paved pathway that's perfect for pushing strollers or biking. A broad avenue called The Great Highway runs between the beach and Golden Gate Park. In the park, there is a three-mile-long paved pathway that joins the bike path around Lake Merced.

When it's warm and sunny, the beach is packed with people enjoying the pleasant ocean views and soft sand. Some prefer coming to the beach later in the day to snack and listen to music in their cars while enjoying the beautiful sunset. Most days you will see experienced surfers riding the waves. Keep your kids away from the water. This beach is unsafe for swimming or wading because of the rough surf, treacherous undertow and strong, unpredictable currents. Even so, children will find oodles of other activities.

SEASONS AND TIMES
→ Year-round: Daily, dawn—dusk.

COST
→ Free.

GETTING THERE
→ By car, from downtown, take Geary Blvd. west. It becomes Point Lobos Ave. then the Great Hwy. as you follow the road south at Cliff House. Or, take Market St. southwest (it becomes Portola Dr.) to Sloat Blvd. and drive west to the Great Hwy. Free parking on site. About 30 minutes from downtown.

→ By public transit, take Muni buses 18 or 48.

NEARBY
→ Lake Merced, Fort Funston, Golden Gate Park, Beach Chalet and Cliff House.

COMMENT
→ Bring jackets if foggy or windy.

Make It a Day Trip
POINT REYES NATIONAL SEASHORE

Point Reyes Station, off Sir Francis Drake, San Rafael
(415) 663-1092
www.nps.gov/pore

Point Reyes, just 30 miles northwest of San Francisco, is a crown jewel in the National Seashore system. Make your first stop at Bear Valley Visitor Center (415-663-1092) to get maps and itineraries. Also featured are beautifully designed walk-through dioramas with interactive exhibits explaining the world of Point Reyes. Be sure you ask about the Junior Ranger program for kids—it can be completed in an afternoon. Next, get ready to hit the trails. Easy ones for families are Earthquake Trail, which takes you along the San Andreas Fault, or Woodpecker Nature Trail that goes past the Morgan Horse Ranch (415-663-1763) and Kule Loklo, a replica of a Coast Miwok village.

If beaching is your thing, hop in your car. Point Reyes' numerous sandy beaches are only a short drive away. Wade close to shore and don't let your children go swimming—the hammering surf, rip currents and undertow are hazardous. At Drakes Beach you'll find a café and the Kenneth C. Patrick Visitor Center (415-669-1250), with information and exhibits about the area. Don't miss the popular Point Reyes Lighthouse (415-669-1534) with its impressive view. On most days kids will observe sea lions basking on offshore rocks, and from January to April see migrating gray whales.

SEASONS AND TIMES
➤ Beaches and Bear Valley trails: Year-round, daily, dawn—dusk. Bear Valley Visitor Center: Year-round, Mon—Fri, 9 am—5 pm; Sat—Sun and holidays, 8 am—5 pm. Ken Patrick Visitor Center: Mid-May—late Aug, Fri—Tue and holidays, 10 am—5 pm. All other times: Sat—Sun and holidays, 10 am—5 pm. Lighthouse Visitor Center: Year-round, Thu—Mon, 10 am—4:30 pm.

COST
➤ Free.

GETTING THERE
➤ By car, take U.S. 101 N. across the Golden Gate Bridge to San Rafael. Take the Sir Francis Drake Exit and drive west. Free parking on site. About 1 hour from downtown.

NEARBY
➤ Tomales Bay State Park, Samuel P. Taylor State Park.

COMMENT
➤ Bring long pants and sweatshirts for the fog and wind, cameras for the wildlife and views, and towels and toys for the beach. The only food in the park is at the restaurant/café at Drakes Beach, though you can eat in Inverness or Olema.

From Marshes to Mud Flats
SAN FRANCISCO BAY NATIONAL WILDLIFE REFUGE

Visitor Center, 1 Marshlands Rd., Fremont (510) 792-0222
Education Center, 1751 Grand Blvd.,
Alviso (408) 262-5513
http://pacific.fws.gov/sfbnwr/

America's first urban wildlife refuge is sure to be a hit with anyone who loves nature. This pristine area is the year-round home for an amazing variety of wildlife. Other species visit during their fall and spring migration.

Boasting 43,000 acres and 25 miles of shoreline, the refuge offers plenty for families to do. Hiking and biking trails and boardwalks wind through salt ponds, marshes, mud flats and sloughs where ground squirrels, cottontail rabbits and gray foxes reside. Stop and listen for the peeps, cracks, chirps and warbles. These calls lead to sandpipers, snowy egrets, ducks, kites, pelicans and, if you are lucky, great blue herons. All kinds of lizards and snakes live here too, as do endangered species such as the salt-marsh harvest mouse.

The Visitor Center on the hill above the parking lot is equipped with interactive exhibits, videos and books on nature and wildlife for kids and adults. You will also find heaps of information on other National Refuges that you can visit in the Bay Area. Don't miss the observation deck with even more nature displays.

SEASONS AND TIMES
→ Park: Year-round, daily, dawn—dusk. Visitor Center: Year-round, Tue—Sun, 10 am—5 pm. Education Center: Year-round, Sat—Sun, 10 am—5 pm.

COST
→ Free.

GETTING THERE
→ By car, take U.S. 101 S. to Redwood City. Access Hwy. 84 (Bayfront Expy.) and take it across the Bay to Paseo Padre Pkwy. Look for signs to Marshlands Rd. Exit and follow Marshlands to the wildlife refuge. Free parking on site. About 45 minutes from downtown.

COMMENT
→ Bring snacks, drinks or pack a picnic. There are no restaurants. Binoculars are a good idea. Nature videos, such as *Who did the Owl Eat?* can be borrowed at no charge at the Visitor Center.

CHAPTER 10

HISTORICAL SITES

Introduction

C ompared to Asia, Europe or even the east coast of the United States, the Bay Area seems very young. The first Spanish ship didn't enter San Francisco Bay until 1775 and the oldest building, Mission Dolores, only dates back to 1782. Still there's lots of history around the Bay that's interesting and fun to investigate. And to kids, most of it will seem ancient.

It shouldn't be surprising that five of the eleven destinations in this chapter are ships—the Spanish founded San Francisco because of its potential as a port. As a result, much of the city's history is intertwined with maritime activities. Other sites in this book, Alcatraz (page 15), the Golden Gate Bridge (page 20) and Fisherman's Wharf (page 18) are historically significant and tied to the Bay.

Read on to learn about some of San Francisco's other kid-friendly historical sites. This chapter includes visiting a 19th-century fort, exploring the home of the "father" of our National Parks, hiking the San Andreas Fault, investigating a Miwok village, playing vintage arcades, learning about San Francisco's maritime history and more. No matter which of these sites you take your kids to, they'll love learning about San Francisco's colorful past and will ask for more.

Old-fashioned Fun
CLIFF HOUSE, MUSÉE MECHANIQUE AND CAMERA OBSCURA

1090 Point Lobos Ave., San Francisco
(415) 556-8642 (Cliff House Visitor Center), (415) 386-1170
(Musée Mechanique), (415) 750-0415 (Camera Obscura)
www.cliffhouse.com/history/history.htm

One of San Francisco's most popular attractions, Cliff House doesn't really qualify as a historical site. The main structure, with a restaurant and Visitor Center, only dates back to 1909. But the charm of the place, perched above the roaring surf, and the Musée Mechanique and Camera Obscura make this destination worth the visit.

Stop at the Visitor Center and see archival photographs of Cliff House's various incarnations. There are also pictures of historic Sutro Baths (visit the ruins just north of Cliff House) and exhibits on the region's natural history. Kids are eager to visit the Musée Mechanique. It houses a grand collection of vintage music boxes and coin-operated amusements. Truly from another era, the mechanical devices are operational and delight kids of all ages with quirky designs, strange jerky movements and finely crafted figures.

Save visiting Camera Obscura for a clear day. You'll want to have a good view of the seals and surf.

This camera doesn't record pictures like a normal one does. It reflects images using a rotating mirror, two lenses and a parabolic dish. This model reproduces Leonardo da Vinci's original design and was built in 1949 as a graduate student thesis project.

SEASONS AND TIMES

➤ Cliff House Visitor Center: Year-round, daily, 10 am—5 pm. Musée Mechanique: Year-round, Mon—Fri, 11 am—7 pm; Sat—Sun and holidays, 10 am—7 pm. Camera Obscura: Year-round, daily, 11 am—sunset.

COST

➤ Musée Mechanique: Free. Amusements take coins. Cliff House Visitor Center: Free. Camera Obscura: Adults $1, children (2 to 12) $0.50, under 2 free.

GETTING THERE

➤ By car, from downtown, take Geary Blvd. west, which becomes Point Lobos Ave. just a couple of blocks before Cliff House. Cliff House is situated where Point Lobos curves south and becomes The Great Highway. Free parking lot nearby or street parking. About 30 minutes from downtown.

➤ By public transit, take Muni bus 18 to Cliff House.

NEARBY

➤ Ocean Beach, San Francisco Zoo, The Coastal Trail.

COMMENT

➤ Plan a 1- to 2-hour visit. Combine your visit with a walk along Ocean Beach or hike The Coastal Trail.

A *San Francisco Classic*
COIT TOWER

**Telegraph Hill Blvd. at Greenwich St., San Francisco
(415) 362-0808**

One of San Francisco's most renowned landmarks, Coit Tower was completed in 1933 and was a gift to the city from wealthy heiress, Lillie Hitchcock Coit. The 210-foot tower is said to resemble the nozzle of a fire hose—the choice of design presumably based on Coit's fascination with firefighting. The tower is dedicated as a monument to the city's volunteer firefighters.

As you might guess, the view from the observation tower is absolutely breathtaking. Walking around the deck you take in the Golden Gate and Bay bridges, Alcatraz and Marin, Berkeley and downtown San Francisco. On a clear day you might also get a glimpse of Mount Saint Helena to the north or Mount Diablo in Contra Costa County to the east. Before these sights however, you'll find yourselves engaged by the depression-era murals decorating the interior entrance of the tower. The artwork depicts life, work and industry in California. Captions identify contemporary figures (and sometimes the artists themselves) in the pieces and give a vibrant sense of the struggles of the times. Most kids aren't interested in the art or the era it portrays. They just want to ride the elevator to the observation deck.

SEASONS AND TIMES
➤ Year-round: Daily, 10 am—6 pm.

COST
➤ Free to view murals. Observation deck: Adults $3.75, seniors (65 and over) $2.50, children (6 to 12) $1.50, under 6 free.

GETTING THERE
➤ By car, take Hwy. 101 N. (Van Ness Ave.) to Bay St. Turn east on Bay to Powell St. and head south. Turn east onto Lombard St. and follow it to Telegraph Hill Blvd. and Pioneer Park. Parking is extremely limited. About 15 minutes from downtown.
➤ By public transit, take Muni bus 39 to Coit Tower.

NEARBY
➤ Pier 39, Fisherman's Wharf, The Embarcadero.

COMMENT
➤ Plan an 1-hour visit. Surrounding the tower is a small but lovely park with snack vendors. Consider combining this with attractions at Pier 39 or Fisherman's Wharf.

Guarding the Bay
FORT POINT NATIONAL HISTORIC SITE

At the termination of Marine Dr., San Francisco
(415) 556-1663
www.nps.gov/fopo

Movie buffs might recognize this site from Alfred Hitchcock's *Vertigo*, or *Bicentennial Man* starring Robin Williams. The U.S. Army Corps of Engineers built Fort Point (the only brick fort west of the Mississippi) between 1853 and 1861. It was used to guard San Francisco and the Bay against possible invasion. Adopting the military strategy of the day, the area was leveled (through massive blasting) so cannons could be positioned at water level. The final structure is set just 15 feet above sea level.

Kids love wandering the massive fort. They visit the powder magazines, storerooms, jail, kitchens and barracks. Each section is identified. For an extra fee, take the audio tour. At the gun emplacements, children can sit on the cannons and peer through the casemate at modern-day ships entering and leaving the Bay. It gives them a small sense of what life was like for the gunnery soldiers of the day. The garrison's quarters—protected by five-foot thick walls—feature historic photographs and other displays from the era.

SEASONS AND TIMES
➺ Year-round: Daily, 10 am—5 pm.

COST
➺ Free.

GETTING THERE
➺ By car, take Hwy. 101 N. (Van Ness Ave.) to Lombard St. Go west on Lombard (you'll still be on Hwy. 101) and continue on as it merges into Presidio Blvd. and then Lincoln Blvd. Take the Long Ave. fork (north). Long becomes Marine Dr.; continue to the very end. Free parking near the Fort. About 20 minutes from downtown.
➺ By public transit, take Muni bus 29. It's a short walk from the closest stop to the Fort.

NEARBY
➤ Golden Gate Bridge, Cliff House, Baker Beach, Golden Gate Promenade.

COMMENT
➤ Plan a 1- to 2-hour visit. Bring a picnic if the weather is good. Directly overhead looms the Golden Gate Bridge. A trail leads to it, though the trek might be too much for younger children.

Home of a Legend
JOHN MUIR NATIONAL HISTORIC SITE

4202 Alhambra Ave., Martinez
(925) 228-8860
www.nps.gov/jomu

John Muir was a Scottish-born naturalist, explorer and writer who immigrated to the United States in 1849 and settled in California in 1868. Many regard him as the father of our National Parks. You can visit his home, gardens and historic surroundings—all lovingly preserved in his memory. After viewing the informative film about Muir's life and work, wander around the house. It's filled with furniture and other family possessions, giving visitors a good understanding of the era. Outside you can visit the fruit orchards and hike to the summit of Mount Wanda. The trail is easy and there's a lovely view of the surrounding Alhambra Valley.

This 325-acre green space also boasts Martinez Adobe—an authentic hacienda built around 1844 that Muir's family occupied. It's open for inspection. Smaller children will be more interested in the gardens and nature trails than in exploring the houses and their history. Try to schedule your visit during good weather so they can be outdoors.

SEASONS AND TIMES
➤ Year-round: Wed—Sun, 10 am—4:30 pm.

COST
➤ Adults $2, children (under 17) free.

GETTING THERE
➤ By car, take I-80 north/east to Hwy. 4 (John Muir Pkwy.). Head east on Hwy. 4 to the Alhambra Ave. Exit. Turn north under the freeway and continue on Alhambra to the park entrance. Free parking on site. About 15 to 20 minutes from I-80.

COMMENT
➤ Plan a 1- to 1 1/2-hour visit. Picnicking locations are nearby.

Natural History
KULE LOKLO AND EARTHQUAKE TRAIL

Point Reyes National Seashore, (off Hwy. 1),
west of Olema
(415) 663-1092 (Bear Valley Visitor Center)
www.nps.gov/pore/resources/cultural/miwok.htm

One of the area's natural treasures, Point Reyes National Seashore (page 170) ranks as a not-to-be-missed outdoor destination. Whether you come to hike, play in the tide pools, bird watch or picnic, make sure you include Kule Loklo and the Earthquake Trail. These attractions are just a short walk from Bear Valley Visitor Center.

Kule Loklo means "Bear Valley" in the Coastal Miwok language. A replica of an ancient Miwok village, it comprises a sweat lodge, a granary and a family dwelling. The buildings were built using authentic materials and tools and can be explored. On many weekends, the Miwok Archeological Preserve of Marin (MAPOM) conducts classes introducing visitors to such Native skills as flint knapping arrowheads, tule basketry and traditional uses of plants. The sessions are for adults, but most children enjoy watching for awhile.

Next, hit the Earthquake Trail. This one-mile self-guided hike takes you along the San Andreas Fault to the epicenter of the Great Earthquake of 1906. Informative signs explain what happened. For example, you'll read about the nearby road moving 24 feet and how a local farmer perpetrated the hoax that the earthquake had swallowed his cow. A widely published picture showed its tail sticking out of the ground. It was later learned the animal had died of natural causes before the 'quake.

SEASONS AND TIMES
➤ Year-round: Daily, sunrise—sunset.

COST
➤ Free.

GETTING THERE
➤ By car, take Hwy. 101 N. to the Central San Rafael Exit and merge onto Irwin St. Turn west onto 3rd St. (it merges into 2nd St., then 4th St., then Red Hill Ave., then Sir Francis Drake Blvd.). Continue on Drake about 17 miles until it ends at Hwy. 1. Turn north on Hwy. 1 to Bear Valley Rd., then head west to the park entrance. Follow the signs to Bear Valley Visitor Center parking lot. About 45 minutes from downtown.

COMMENT
➤ Combine these sites with a visit to the beach or a hike along Bear Valley Trail. Plan to spend the day.

This Old House
MISSION DOLORES

**3321 - 16th St., San Francisco
(415) 621-8203
http://missiondolores.citysearch.com**

Mission Dolores—properly called the Mission San Francisco de Assisi—is not just the oldest building in San Francisco. It is the sixth of the state's missions and embodies the Spanish settlement of California in the 18th century. Completed in 1791, the building's four-foot thick adobe walls were strong enough to withstand the 1906 earthquake, leaving the city with a remarkable landmark.

Visitors can take a self-guided tour of the Mission. Brochures explaining its historical significance are located near the entrance. Take time to examine the altar and other artifacts that represent another era and a different world. The ceiling, now restored and repainted, was originally the work of local Ohlone Natives. Their vibrant designs add a powerful element to a fascinating building.

For older kids, the highlight may well be the cemetery that lies alongside the Mission. Many of San Francisco's streets are named after some of the graveyard's eminent residents. A few of the city's more notorious characters lie alongside them. Younger children who tire of the visit will enjoy visiting Mission Dolores Park, a few blocks south of the Mission.

SEASONS AND TIMES
➤ Summer: May—Sept, 9 am—4:30 pm. Winter: Oct—Apr, 9 am—4 pm. Closed major holidays.

COST
➤ Adults $3, children (5 to 18) $2, under 5 free.

GETTING THERE
➤ By car, from downtown, take Market St. southwest to Dolores St. Turn south to 16th St. The Mission is on the southwest corner at the intersection of Dolores and 16th. Metered street parking. About 15 minutes from downtown.
➤ By public transit, take BART to the 16th St. Station and walk west a few blocks on 16th. Or, take Muni bus 22 or Muni Metro J to the Mission.

NEARBY
➤ Mission Dolores Park.

COMMENT
➤ Allow an hour to wander the chapel and grounds. Lots of great Mexican and Central American restaurants are in the vicinity.

Our Maritime Roots
SAN FRANCISCO MARITIME NATIONAL HISTORIC PARK

Hyde St. Pier (at Hyde on Jefferson St.)
Museum (intersection of Beach and Polk streets),
San Francisco
(415) 556-3002
www.maritime.org

If you like looking at historic vessels and displays with nautical themes, San Francisco Maritime National Historic Park is the place to do it. Comprising the Museum and Hyde Street Pier, the Historic Park is very popular with local residents who come back again and again.

The Museum building is memorable, not just for its video panels and interactive exhibits, but also for its "modernist" WPA architecture. Kids with a keen interest in maritime history will enjoy exploring the exhibits. Others will be eager to visit Hyde Street Pier. One of the largest collections of historic maritime ships in the world is moored there. The star of the show is *Balclutha*, an 1886 fully rigged tall ship. You'll also see *Eureke*, an 1890 San Francisco ferry; *Alma*, an 1891 scow schooner; *C.A. Thayer*, an 1895 lumber schooner; *Hercules*, a 1907 ocean tug boat; *Wapama*, a 1915 steam schooner; *Eppleton Hall*, a 1914 river tug and over 100 smaller craft. Most represent the kind of vessels that were commonly seen in the Bay around 1900.

Kids can climb aboard the ships and inspect them. Friendly attendants explain how each ship was built and describe a bit of its history—such as the type of work it performed.

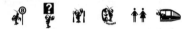

SEASONS AND TIMES
➤ Museum: Year-round, daily, 10 am—5 pm. Hyde St. Pier: Summer (May 15—Sept 15), daily, 9:30 am—5:30 pm. In winter the pier closes at 5 pm. Closed on major holidays.

COST
➤ Museum: Free. Hyde St. Pier: Adults $5, seniors (over 62) and youths (12 to 17) $2, under 12 are free with an adult.

GETTING THERE
➤ By car, from The Embarcadero, take North Point St. west to Hyde St. (for the pier), or Polk St. (for the museum.) Limited street parking. Pay lots are nearby. Walk north towards the waterfront. About 15 minutes from The Embarcadero.
➤ By public transit, take Muni buses 19, 30 or 42 or the Powell-Hyde cable car to the pier.

NEARBY
➤ Ghirardelli Square, The Cannery, Fisherman's Wharf, USS *Pampanito*.

COMMENT
➤ Many kids zoom through the Museum building in 30 minutes, while the carefully preserved ships at Hyde Street Pier absorb them for a couple of hours.

Full Steam Ahead
SS JEREMIAH O'BRIEN

Pier 45 (at Taylor St.), San Francisco
(415) 441-3101
www.maritime.org/hnsa-job.htm

Have ye ever been to sea? Here's your chance. Two times a year the SS *Jeremiah O'Brien* steams through the Gate and up the coast on an all-day excursion. What makes the trip memorable is that *Jeremiah O'Brien* is the only vessel to remain operating from the Liberty shipbuilding program during World War II. Then, about 2,700 cargo steamers like her were constructed to carry troops and supplies to Europe and Asia. *Jeremiah O'Brien* sailed to Canada, the United Kingdom, South America, Australia and the Philippines. In 1994, she steamed to Normandy to participate in the 50th anniversary of the Allied invasion.

At other times, you can wander the decks of this historic ship. A self-guided tour map leads you to the engine room, bridge, radio room, berthing quarters and mess hall. "Crew" docents explain the workings of the ship and a little of her history. During Steaming Weekends, which are held two times each month, you can see her engines operate.

SEASONS AND TIMES
➤ Year-round: Daily, 9 am—4 pm. Call for dates of Steaming Weekends and all-day excursions.

COST

➤ Adults $5, children (6 to 18) $3, under 6 free. The all-day cruises are $100 per person.

GETTING THERE

➤ By car, follow The Embarcadero to Pier 45. There are pay lots in the area and limited street parking. About 5 minutes from downtown.
➤ By public transit, take Muni buses 19, 30 or 42, or Muni Metro F. The Powell-Hyde and Powell-Mason cable cars stop a short walk away.

NEARBY

➤ USS *Pampanito*, San Francisco Maritime National Historical Park, Ghirardelli Square, The Cannery, Fisherman's Wharf.

COMMENT

➤ Plan a 1-hour visit aboard the SS *Jeremiah O'Brien*. You can spend the whole day in the area.

Space Ship
USS *HORNET* MUSEUM

Pier 3, Alameda Point, Alameda
(510) 521-8448
www.uss-hornet.org

O ne of the most decorated aircraft carriers from War World II welcomes you aboard. USS *Hornet* served for 16 continuous months in the Pacific Ocean combat zone. You can explore the massive flight deck and hangars on this awesome craft. The visit also includes the bridge on the island superstructure, the berthing areas and mess halls. Guides will be your leaders and tell you about the ship's operations. For example, you will learn how planes took off and landed on the flight deck. A number of historic aircraft are displayed.

But that's not all. In 1969 the *Hornet* was the recovery vessel for the Apollo 11 and Apollo 12 moon missions. Kids love learning where the returning astronauts took their first steps back on earth. They get to see where the Mobile Quarantine Facility stood. Astronauts lived in this house trailer upon their return from the moon to prevent possible contamination by otherworldly bacteria.

SEASONS AND TIMES
➤ Year-round: Daily, 10 am—5 pm. Closes Tue at 1:30 pm.

COST
➤ Adults $12, seniors (over 64), active military and students with ID $10, youths (5 to 18) $5, under 5 free.

GETTING THERE
➤ By car, from the Bay Bridge, take Hwy. 880 S. and exit at Broadway/Alameda. Turn north on 5th St. Merge into the left lane and follow signs to Alameda via the Webster St. Tube. Upon exiting the tube follow Webster to Atlantic Ave. and turn north. Follow Atlantic through the gate into Alameda Point. Turn west on Ferry Point and proceed along the water to USS *Hornet*. Free parking on site. About 15 to 20 minutes from the bridge.
➤ By public transit, take BART to the 12th St. Station in downtown Oakland and transfer to AC Transit bus 10 (it operates 6 am—6 pm) and ride it to the *Hornet*'s pier. Or, disembark BART at the Fruitvale Station in Oakland and transfer to AC Transit bus 50 (5:30 am—9 pm). It stops about 500 yards from the ship.

NEARBY
➤ Crab Cove, Oakland Museum, Lake Merritt.

COMMENT
➤ Plan a 2-hour visit.

Dive! Dive!
USS PAMPANITO

Pier 45 (at Taylor St.), San Francisco
(415) 351-3105
www.maritime.org

Here's a visit everyone will be talking about long after it's over—a tour through a submarine. The USS *Pampanito*, a 312-foot submarine that saw combat in World War II, is open for inspection. You'll find her a few blocks east of Hyde Street Pier in the heart of Fisherman's Wharf.

A self-guided audio tour gives you information and insights on submarine life. You'll learn about the specific functions that took place in each area of the ship. Not even the tiniest apartment compares to the compressed environment of a submarine. Kids and adults are always amazed to see the crew's sleeping berths perched atop torpedoes and a single narrow passage that runs the length of the ship.

SEASONS AND TIMES
➤ Summer (May 31—early Oct): Daily, 9 am—8 pm. (Closes Wed at 6 pm). Winter (early Oct—May 31): Sun—Thu, 9 am—6 pm. Fri—Sat, 9 am—8 pm.

COST
➤ Adults $7, seniors (over 62) $5, children (6 to 12) and active duty military with ID $4, under 6 free. Family pass (2 adults and up to 4 kids under 18) $20. Self-guided audio tour included in ticket price.

GETTING THERE
➤ By car, from The Embarcadero, go west on Jefferson St. and immediately begin to look for street parking (very limited). There are pay lots (expensive) in the area. About 15 minutes from downtown.
➤ By public transit, take Muni buses 19, 30 or 42, or Muni Metro F. The Powell-Hyde and Powell-Mason cable cars stop a short walk away.

NEARBY
➤ SS *Jeremiah O'Brien*, San Francisco Maritime National Historical Park, Ghirardelli Square, The Cannery, Fisherman's Wharf.

COMMENT
➤ It only takes 30 minutes to tour the sub, but you can spend the whole day in the area. Wear sturdy shoes for climbing ladders.

The Floating White House
USS POTOMAC

**Franklin Delano Roosevelt Pier, (at Clay St. off The Embarcadero), Oakland
(510) 627-1215 or (510) 839-8256 (information line)
www.usspotomac.org**

Built as a Coast Guard Cutter, USS *Potomac* became Franklin D. Roosevelt's "floating White House" in 1936. A beautiful vessel in its own right, you can tour the craft, sit in the stern where the President entertained visiting dignitaries and examine his cabin in detail. Of particular interest is the hand-operated elevator hidden inside a false smokestack. Roosevelt used this to hoist himself between the saloon and upper boat deck (polio caused paralysis in his lower body.)

To learn more about Roosevelt and *Potomac*, go on the two-hour family history cruise. Four times a month (between March and November), the ship cruises San Francisco's waterfront and around Treasure Island.

SEASONS AND TIMES
➤ Dockside tours: Wed and Fri, 10 am—2 pm; Sun, noon—4 pm. History cruises: Mid-Mar—mid-Nov, first and third Thursdays and second and fourth Saturdays of each month.

COST
➤ Dockside tours: Adults $3, seniors (over 60) $2, youths (6 to 17) $1, under 6 free. Family rate (2 adults and children under age 18) $5. History cruises: Adults $30, seniors (over 60) $27, youths (6 to 17) $15, under 6 free.

GETTING THERE
➤ By car, take Hwy. 880 S. to the Jackson St. Exit. Go west on Jackson to Second St. and turn north. Continue on to Broadway. Go west on Broadway until The Embarcadero. Turn south to Clay St. Street parking nearby and in pay lots. About 15 to 20 minutes from I-880.
➤ By public transit, take AC Transit buses A, 58, 59/59A or 88 to Clay St. and Second St., about 2 blocks from the pier.

NEARBY
➤ Jack London Square, Yoshi's, Oakland Museum, USS *Hornet*.

COMMENT
➤ Plan a 1-hour visit and take in some of the other attractions in the area.

CHAPTER 11

GETTING THERE IS HALF THE FUN

Introduction

Sometimes the journey is just as important as the destination—traveling on a ferry or by train can provide all the entertainment your kids need for one day. Even if it's only the means to an end, the way you get there often adds a wonderful dimension to an outing. The suggestions in this chapter get you out of your car. Naturally, the Bay is prominently featured in these excursions. Going on a Bay cruise or embarking on a journey in a real sailboat is a special experience for children. But there's more to San Francisco than the Bay. Have you ridden on the city's world-famous cable cars or charming old-time streetcars? Take those aspiring stairmasters to try out the Filbert and Greenwich Steps. Also listed are some scenic and popular recreational pathways—San Francisco has its share of these—where you can bike, in-line skate or simply push a stroller, and always be within sight of the water. There's also information about the Bay Area's widespread network of public transportation. Think of this as a start to many fun ways of getting around.

All Aboard!
AMTRAK CAPITOL EXPRESS AND CALIFORNIA STATE RAILROAD MUSEUM

(800) USA-RAIL (872-7245) (Amtrak)
www.amtrakcapitols.com
(916) 445-6645 (California State Railroad Museum)
www.csrmf.org

Riding Amtrak's *Capitol Express* to the California State Railroad Museum in Sacramento offers a special thrill for train lovers. Even those mildly entertained by trains enjoy this excursion. Catch the *Capitol Express* in Oakland (245 – 2nd Ave.), Emeryville (5885 Landregan St.) or Berkeley (University Ave. at 3rd St.), or ride the Amtrak shuttle bus from San Francisco (at the Ferry Building, 31 The Embarcadero) to the Emeryville station. The *Capitol Express* makes seven round trips daily.

It's about a two-hour trip to Sacramento from the East Bay. On the journey kids can visit the dining car for snacks, amble up and down the aisles, gaze out the windows at beautiful scenery, read or play games. Amtrak's trains offer comfortable seating and social areas with tables, perfect for families.

From the Sacramento station, it's only a block or two walk to Old Sacramento, site of the Railroad

Museum (2nd and I streets) and the charming but touristy historic district. At the Railroad Museum, visitors are welcome to climb aboard historic locomotives, passenger cars and Pullman sleepers. Compare your "luxury" ride with the great steam trains of the 19th century.

SEASONS AND TIMES
➤ *Capitol Express:* Year-round, daily. Call for departure times. Railroad Museum: Year-round, daily, 10 am–5 pm.

COST
➤ *Capitol Express:* Adults $14 (one way from Berkeley, Emeryville or Oakland stations, add $1 for feeder bus from San Francisco), children (2 to 15) half-price (2 children allowed per adult for discount), under 2 free. Railroad Museum: Adults $3, youths (under 17) free.

GETTING THERE
➤ Call Amtrak for directions to the station nearest you, or check the website above.

Enjoy the Day on the Bay
BAY CRUISES

BLUE & GOLD FLEET
Pier 41 (Docks), Pier 39 (Ticket office), San Francisco
(415) 773-1188
www.blueandgoldfleet.com

RED & WHITE FLEET
Pier 43 - 1/2 (at the foot of Taylor St.), San Francisco
(415) 673-2900
www.redandwhite.com

S ince swimming in the frigid San Francisco Bay is unthinkable, taking a boat cruise is about as close as most people get to the water. The Blue & Gold Fleet and The Red & White Fleet operate sightseeing cruises in the Bay. Each offers a variety of packages for families, taking in all the highpoints with lively commentary. Even the one-hour excursion is something your family will remember for a long time. Being out on the water, sailing around Alcatraz (page 15) and looking up at the Golden Gate Bridge (page 20), cruising past Angel Island (page 139) and Sausalito provides a sense of adventure and romance that everyone enjoys.

One word of caution: small children (and adults too) can find rough water frightening. Schedule your cruise for good weather. Sheltered as it is, on a windy day the Bay can be choppy. Bring sweaters or jackets for everyone; it can get cool.

SEASONS AND TIMES
➤ Year-round: Daily. Call or visit the websites for departure times.

COST
➤ Blue & Gold: Adults $17, seniors (62 and up) and youths (12 to 18) $13, children (5 to 11) $9. Red & White: Adults $18, seniors (60 and up) and youths (12 to 18) $14, children (5 to 11) $10.

GETTING THERE
For both Blue & Gold and Red & White:
➤ By car, from downtown, take The Embarcadero north to Pier 39. Parking is available at the Pier 39 lot, or on the adjacent streets. About 15 minutes from downtown.

➤ By public transit, take Muni buses 30, 32 or 42. Or take the Muni Metro (F line) to Fisherman's Wharf.

NEARBY
➤ Fisherman's Wharf, San Francisco Maritime National Historical Park, USS *Pampanito*, Frequent Flyers bungee trampoline attraction, SS *Jeremiah O'Brien*.

COMMENT
➤ Combine your 1-hour Bay Cruise with the amusements at Pier 39 and Fisherman's Wharf, or the historic ships at Hyde Street Pier.

Cruising Along
BAY FERRIES

www.transitinfo.com

One of the great things about the Bay Area is the Bay itself. Getting out on the water is an easy adventure. Just hop on one of the ferries that connects San Francisco to East Bay or North Bay; kids have a great time. Whether you are sailing to Sausalito from San Francisco or to San Francisco from the East Bay, the views are spectacular. Other pluses include the sea birds, salty air, chugging of the ferry and the thrill of being off the roads and bridges. Be it a day of sightseeing or just an outing with the family, taking the ferry certainly does make getting there more than half the fun.

The Blue & Gold Ferry
(415) 705-5555 (Schedules and fares)

Connects Oakland and Alameda to San Francisco. About a 30-minute trip. The Alameda dock is at Gateway Center (2991 Main St.). The Oakland dock is at the foot of Clay Street in Jack London Square. Ferries dock in San Francisco at the Ferry Building (Market St. and The Embarcadero), or at Pier 41 in Fisherman's Wharf. The Blue & Gold Fleet also runs a ferry connecting downtown Sausalito with Pier 41.

Golden Gate Ferry Service
(415) 257-4563 (Schedules and fares)

Connects Larkspur with San Francisco (50 minutes) and Sausalito to San Francisco (30 minutes). Commuters use these boats weekday mornings and evenings. They are great fun for kids at other times.

The Wheels on the Bus Go Round and Round
BUS TOURS

Nothing beats a bus tour if you want an overview of San Francisco's major attractions. Gray Line offers visitors and people new to the city narrated tours, ranging from a couple of hours taking in all the high points, to all-day trips to Monterey. Try the Trolley Hop Tour. It lasts about 90 minutes and kids love the colorful buses resembling San Francisco's cable cars and trolleys. Buses leave from Union Square, Pier 39 and Pier 43 and make a loop around the downtown area. Your ticket is good for the entire day, so you can get on and off at any of the scheduled stops. Grab a bite to eat, shop or give the kids a chance blow off steam. Board the next bus or the one after that—they arrive at regular intervals. Gray Line's Motorized Cable Car Tour lasts three hours and goes to Fort Point, the Golden Gate Bridge, Palace of Fine Arts, Japantown and beyond.

The Blue & Gold Fleet offers ferry and motor coach all-day package tours to such sights as Muir

Woods and Six Flags Marine World. The latter attraction is a favorite with kids and is open May through September. Blue & Gold also offers packages that combine San Francisco city bus tours with Bay Cruises, with the option of visiting Alcatraz. The Red & White Fleet offers a similar lineup of tours.

GRAY LINE
(415) 558-9400
www.graylinesanfrancisco.com

➤ Trolley Hop Tour: Adults $15, children (5 to 11) $8. Tours depart every 30 to 45 minutes. Gray Line also has longer tours that combine ferries and coaches.

BLUE & GOLD FLEET
(415) 773-1188
www.blueandgoldfleet.com

RED & WHITE FLEET
(415) 673-2900
www.redandwhite.com

A *Landmark on Wheels*
CABLE CARS

(415) 673-6864
www.sfmuni.com

Your San Francisco experience won't be complete without riding a cable car. Once they make the round trip, kids say "Let's do it again." The feel of the open-air, the rumbling wheels, the precipitous hills and the "clang, clang, clang" of the trolley are all part of the fun.

Designated National Historic Landmarks in 1964, cable cars have operated in the city since 1873. San Francisco boasts three cable car lines: Powell-Mason, Powell-Hyde and California Street. The Powell-Mason and Powell-Hyde lines, which begin their routes where Market and Powell streets intersect, cross Nob Hill. The Mason car terminates next to the Hyde Street Pier and Ghirardelli Square (page 18). The Hyde Street car stops about three blocks from Fisherman's Wharf (page 18). The California Street car travels along California Street from Market Street and across Chinatown to Van Ness Avenue. You get on or off the cars anywhere along the way. Ticket dispensers are located at the start and end of each line, or pay the conductor wherever you board.

Each line has a stop at the Cable Car Museum (page 35). Seeing the cables and gears that drive the system adds a whole new dimension to your ride.

SEASONS AND TIMES
➤ Year-round: Daily. Cars operate every 6 to 12 minutes (time and day dependent) from 6 am until 12:45 am. First and last departures vary by line.

COST
➤ Individuals (5 and older) $2, under 5 ride free. Fares are one-way only. No transfers.

GETTING THERE
➤ Avoid riding the cable cars during commute hours if possible. Many San Francisco tourist attractions are near the cable car lines making riding them part of the outing.

Get a Leg Up
FILBERT AND GREENWICH STEPS

Filbert and Greenwich streets, San Francisco

Here's a chance to combine your adventurous side with a little exercise, while pretending you are a local. San Francisco is renowned for its hills, but Telegraph Hill with Coit Tower (page 179) perched atop is probably the quintessential example. While you can drive to the top or take a bus, you miss half the fun of the visit. Implanted on the east side of the steep rocky Telegraph Hill are two amazing sets of stairs that are accessed from Filbert and Greenwich streets. They are not the straight up and down variety. These stairs wander this way and that on their ascent, allowing you to peek into tiny lanes and storybook residences along the way. Then when you turn around, there are the breathtaking views of the Bay Bridge and East Bay.

The outing may be too much for very young children, but families up for the climb will find it a rewarding experience. A word of caution: parts of the Filbert steps are rickety and wooden. The Greenwich steps are mostly concrete.

SEASONS AND TIMES
→ Year-round: Daily.

COST

➤ Free.

GETTING THERE

➤ By car, from downtown, take The Embarcadero south to Greenwich St. Turn west on Greenwich and drive 1 block to Sansome St. Metered parking is usually available. About 5 minutes from downtown.

➤ By public transit, take the Muni Metro (F line) to Greenwich.

NEARBY

➤ Pier 39, Fisherman's Wharf.

COMMENT

➤ Depending upon your stamina and that of your kids, it takes 20 minutes to climb the steps. Combine your hike with a visit to Coit Tower for a 2- to 3-hour excursion.

Setting Sail on
THE *HAWAIIAN CHIEFTAIN*

Sausalito Marina Plaza, Sausalito
(415) 331-3214
www.hawaiianchieftain.com

Built of steel in 1988, the *Hawaiian Chieftain* is a magnificent 103-foot replica of a 1790s-style tallship. The nautically savvy will recognize her as a square topsail ketch. Others, including most kids, are thrilled just to be on board. A cruise on the *Hawaiian Chieftain* far surpasses the usual boat tour. You're on a real sailing vessel, with the prevailing winds and tides determining which route the ship follows. There are backup engines if required.

Three different Bay cruises are offered. On Wednesdays, the Sunset Sail features a buffet and views of San Francisco in the evening. On Sundays there's the Brunch Sail. The best cruise for families is the Adventure Sail on Saturdays. Passengers do more than take in the scenery during the Saturday sailing—everyone is encouraged to help at one of the stations. At the helm station, kids steer the boat; at the bracing station they move the yards and learn nautical knots; and at the deck station they get to handle the lines and sails.

In addition to the cruises, the *Hawaiian Chieftain* offers one-hour dockside tours to groups on weekday mornings ($5 per person).

SEASONS AND TIMES

➤ Apr or May—Oct: Sunset Sail, Wed, 6 am—9 pm; Adventure Sail, Sat, 9 am—1 pm; Brunch Sail, Sun, 10 am—1 pm.

COST

➤ Prices vary according to the cruise and range from $40 to $50 for adults and $15 to $25 for children.

GETTING THERE

➤ By car, take U.S. 101 N. across the Golden Gate Bridge. Take the Sausalito/Marin City Exit onto Bridgeway heading south to Harbor Dr. Turn east on Harbor, then south onto Marinship Way. Free parking across from the marina. About 30 minutes from downtown.

➤ By public transit, take Golden Gate buses 2, 10, 20 or 50 from the Transbay Terminal at Mission and 1st streets in San Francisco. Or take the Sausalito ferry and pick up one of the buses from the Sausalito Ferry Terminal.

NEARBY

➤ Sausalito, Bay Model Visitor Center.

COMMENT
➤ Dress warmly, preferably in layers. A stroll in Sausalito with a stop for ice cream rounds out a wonderful day.

Getting Around
PUBLIC TRANSPORTATION

W hile mostly businesslike and without frills, the patchwork quilt of public transportation throughout the Bay Area will get you where you want to go inexpensively. Moreover, for many kids the grown-up feel of being on public transit can be a delight in itself. The following are the main providers of public transportation in the Bay Area. For connections that are not covered here, visit www.transitinfo.org.

Bay Area Rapid Transit (BART)
(415) 989-BART (2278)
www.bart.gov

This regional subway/rail system is a great way to get to and from East Bay. It's the travel mode of choice within San Francisco—provided your destination is near the line. Trains are relatively clean and quiet, though crowded during commute hours.

➤ Prices are based on distance traveled. Children under 4 ride free.

San Francisco Municipal Railroad (Muni)
(415) 673-MUNI (6864)
www.sfmuni.com

Muni is the operator for all San Francisco buses, streetcars, cable cars and historic streetcars. The city's buses and shiny metro streetcars get you almost anywhere you want to go in the city. Metro streetcars operate underground in downtown and above ground elsewhere.

➤ Basic fares (buses and metro lines): Adults $1, youths (5 to 17) $0.35, under 5 free. For short-term visitors, 1, 3 and 7-day "passports" provide unlimited rides for a flat fee with discounts at major tourist attractions.

AC Transit
(510) 891-4777
www.actransit.org

The East Bay's primary bus system, AC Transit carries passengers from Richmond in the north to Fremont and Newark in the south. This clean, efficient local service provides transportation to important destinations and tourist attractions throughout the area. AC Transit's service to San Francisco terminates at the Transbay Terminal at First and Mission streets in San Francisco.

➤ Basic fares (local service): Individuals (13 and older) $1.35, children (5 to 12) $0.65, under 5 free. Booklets of 10 tickets available at a discount. Transbay fares: Individuals (13 and older) $2.50, children (12 and under) $1.25.

Golden Gate Transit
(415) 923-2000
www.goldengate.org

In addition to maintaining the Golden Gate Bridge and running the commuter ferries to and from Marin County, the Golden Gate Transit District also operates Golden Gate Transit buses. These buses provide connections to and from Marin and Sonoma counties with additional service to west Contra Costa County.

➟ Fares are zone-based with discounts for youths (6 to 18). Children under 5 ride free.

Caltrain
(800) 660-4287
www.caltrain.com

This popular commuter train serves the Peninsula and South Bay, as far south as Gilroy. Primarily used by commuters, the line features the rumble and romance of traditional trains.

➟ Fares are zone based. One child (under 5) per adult rides free. One child (under 12) per adult rides half fare.

Head Out and Explore the
RECREATIONAL
PATHWAYS

There's more to the Bay Area than hills and water. Lots of great places—both level and beautiful—are perfect for bikers, 'bladers hikers and strollers. Some of the popular sites are described below, with page numbers where more detailed information can be found.

Golden Gate Park, San Francisco (page 22)

San Francisco's glorious Golden Gate Park is the ideal place to bike, push a stroller or in-line skate any day of the week. On Sundays it becomes even better when John F. Kennedy Drive is closed to cars. A festival atmosphere fills the air and whether you're on foot or wheels, there's something exciting about traveling down the middle of the road where autos usually prevail.

Ocean Beach, San Francisco (page 168)

One of San Francisco's favorite strolling and biking spots. Travel along the broad sidewalk with the Pacific Ocean rolling out before you, then play in the sand.

Golden Gate Promenade, San Francisco (page 165)

Behind you is beautiful Aquatic Park. In front of you, a 3.5-mile smooth path leads past Marina Green, Crissy Field, a restored tidal marsh and historic Fort Point. What are you waiting for?

Inspiration Point Trail, Tilden Regional Park, Berkeley (page 153)

On sunny days, hikers, bikers and those out for a stroll line this pathway. It wanders for miles through Berkeley Hills. A few steep hills make the route too rigorous for most in-line skaters. The woodsy feel and dramatic views of the Bay and Golden Gate Bridge explain the popularity of this wonderful trail.

Coyote Point County Recreational Area, San Mateo (page 161)

One of the jewels of the Peninsula, Coyote Point has some excellent recreational paths along the Bay. Once you've worked out some of your restless energy head to the beach or museum.

The Bayshore Trail, Eastshore State Park, Richmond

The Bay Area's newest park stretches along the shore of the Bay from Golden Gate Fields in Albany to the Richmond Marina. A smooth, paved path meanders through restored tidal marshes providing a wonderful place for a gentle bike ride or an easy stroll amid myriad shorebirds.

Ride Back in Time
S. F. MUNI HISTORIC STREETCARS

(415) 673-6864
www.sfmuni.com

In a city with lots of quaint fun, San Francisco's Historic Streetcars (Market & Wharves F line) are a special treat.

The line runs from the intersection of Market and Castro streets, along Market to The Embarcadero, and then north to Fisherman's Wharf. You can ride one of the "modern" cars that were built in the 1930s.

These have been repainted and sport the colors of transportation authorities in cities using cars like these, or board one of the trolleys that were built in Milan, Italy in 1928. There is just enough rumbling and swaying to let you know you've stepped into another era. Inside each car, a panel contains a colorful story about the history of these streetcars, and conductors call out stops along the way. It's a great way to take in the scenery and pure entertainment for the kids.

When you get off at Fisherman's Wharf, everyone is guaranteed to have a smile on their faces.

SEASONS AND TIMES
➤ Year-round: Daily. Cars depart every 6 to 15 minutes (time and day dependent) from 6 am to 12:30 am.

COST
➤ Adults (18 and older) $1, youths (5 to 17) $0.35, under 5 free.

COMMENT
➤ Combine this with Fisherman's Wharf, a climb up Filbert or Greenwich steps to Coit Tower, or any major downtown tourist attraction.

CHAPTER 12

FAVORITE FESTIVALS

Introduction

Week after week, glorious processions of festivals and fairs enliven San Francisco and the surrounding communities. Whether you are looking for colorful ethnic feasts, fireworks spectaculars or street fairs that are just plain fun, you and your family are sure to find something that fulfills your desire.

Some of the most popular and kid-friendly events in the area are described in this chapter. Consider them as "don't miss" favorites. Lots more are included in the Directory of Events at the end of the book. Wherever possible, contact information has been provided so you can get exact dates and details.

While most of the events are free, you will find tempting goodies, fun crafts and a number of extras to entice you to spend a few dollars. Providing heaps of entertainment value for the whole family, these events are a real bargain.

There are Lions and Dragons (oh my!) at
CHINESE NEW YEAR

Grant St. (Chinatown), San Francisco
(415) 982-3000

One of the biggest celebrations in San Francisco's festival calendar, Chinese New Year involves two weeks of colorful events. The Chinese New Year Flower Fair and Chinatown Community Street Fair, two of the most popular for families, feature ethnic food, crafts, music and games for kids. The highlight of the festival is the giant, lively parade that gets underway in the late afternoon following a route from Market and Second streets to Columbus Avenue. It is replete with traditional lion and dragon dances and spectacular Chinese costumes. Get there early and claim your piece of the curbside! Keep in mind, however, that the combination of San Francisco's chilly and rainy winter weather, the noise of firecrackers and the crowds may be overwhelming for younger children.

In conjunction with the annual New Year celebration, the Chinese Culture Center, on the third floor at 750 Kearny Street (415-986-1822; www.c-c-c.org), offers displays, tours, craft demonstrations and performances. For detailed information, contact the Center.

SEASONS AND TIMES

➤ The New Year is calculated on the lunar calendar and usually occurs at the end of January; though this varies from year to year. Call for specific dates and times.

COST

➤ Free.

GETTING THERE

➤ If you drive, there is pay parking at the Sutter-Stockton, St. Mary's Square or Portsmouth Square garages. Keep in mind that traffic is difficult and parking limited.

➤ By public transit, Chinatown is about a 15-minute walk from the Montgomery Street and Powell Street BART stations. From elsewhere in the city, take Muni buses 1, 12 or 15, or ride the cable car that runs along California St.

COMMENT

➤ Pack warm clothing and rain gear for evening festivities. This is one of San Francisco's most flamboyant celebrations. Plan to spend several hours.

A *Taste of Japan*
CHERRY BLOSSOM FESTIVAL

**Japan Center Mall and Japan Center on Post St. between
Laguna St. and Webster St. (Japantown), San Francisco
(415) 563-2313**

A mainstay on the festival calendar for more than 30 years, the Cherry Blossom Festival embraces a spirited parade, drummers, craft exhibits and the rolling of a 40-foot sushi. Your kids will have a great time exploring Japantown and delighting in the rich Japanese cultural heritage on display. There are demonstrations of traditional art from weaving, to karate, to origami. Art and craft booths feature work by local artists who have adapted centuries-old forms to modern uses, such as electrical switch plates covered with Japanese wallpaper. There is music, from traditional to Japanese hip-hop, plus lots to eat (green tea ice cream is a perennial favorite).

The festival kicks off with a parade that proceeds from Civic Center Plaza to Fillmore Street. It boasts unique features such as Akita dogs and breeders, Taiko drummers and Buddhist floats.

SEASONS AND TIMES
➤ Two consecutive weekends in April. Call for specific dates and times.

COST
➤ Free.

GETTING THERE
➤ By car, from downtown, take Geary St. and head east. A 5-minute drive brings you to a garage under Japan Center that is conveniently entered off Geary.
➤ By public transit, take Muni buses 2, 3, 4 or 22.

COMMENT
➤ This is a great family-friendly opportunity. You can observe Japanese cultural traditions and share in them. Plan to spend the better part of a day.

If it is Exotic, it Must Be
CARNAVAL

**Harrison St. (between 16th St. and 22nd St.),
San Francisco
(415) 826-1401
www.meca.bigstep.com**

San Francisco's version of Mardi Gras is one of the city's largest annual public events. Carnaval is held on one day and draws crowds in excess of a quarter million people. There are 30 to 40 contingents of dancers decked out in exotic costumes, including children from local schools who perform along the route.

Within the festival area, two main stages and five mini-stages feature a wide range of live music including reggae, jazz and salsa. There are booths with arts and crafts as well as food and refreshments. A children's area has rides for the younger set.

SEASONS AND TIMES
➤ April or May, depending on the date of Easter. Parade: 10 am–1 pm. Festival: 11 am–6 pm.

COST
➤ Free.

GETTING THERE
➤ Street parking is scarce in the area.
➤ By public transit, take BART to the 16th Street Station. Or take Muni buses 12, 14, 22, 33, 48, 49 or 53.

COMMENT
➤ Faithful in spirit to its Brazilian original, there is a lot of flesh. It may
be inappropriate for those with more conservative tastes. Plan to spend
at least a half-day.

Latin Rhythms and Flavors
CINCO DE MAYO

**24th St. to Mission St. to 20th St. (parade); Civic Center
Plaza (festival), bounded by Grove, McAllister,
Polk and Larkin streets, San Francisco
(415) 826-1401
www.meca.bigstep.com**

Your family will be transported south of the border at this festival. Though officially commemorating a Mexican military victory, the San Francisco Cinco de Mayo parade and festival engages the region's entire Hispanic population. It includes many Central American and Puerto Rican immigrants who call San Francisco's Mission District home and draws participants from all over the Bay Area. Music and dancing abound with the Ballet Folklorico performing regional dances from throughout Mexico. There are Salsa contingents, Aztec dancers and mariachis—a feast for eyes and ears.

Though there is an admission fee to enter the festival site, once inside all the children's activities are free. There is lots to do, especially for youngsters. Rides such as dragon slides and bounce castles are low-key. The arts and crafts booth offers the opportunity to bring home a treasured souvenir. Be sure to sample the array of tasty Latin fare at the food stands.

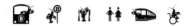

SEASONS AND TIMES
➤ Sunday closest to May 5. Parade: 10 am—noon; festival, 11 am—6 pm.

COST
➤ Parade: Free. Festival site: Individuals $5, seniors $2, under 10 free.

GETTING THERE
➤ Parking is scarce near the parade. For the festival, park in the Civic Center Garage, which is under the Plaza and enters from McAllister St.
➤ By public transit, for the parade, take BART to the 24th Street Station. Or take Muni buses 12, 14, 48, 49 or 67. For the festival, take BART to the Civic Center Station. Or take the Muni Metro (F line) to the Civic Center Station.

COMMENT
➤ This is the largest of many Cinco de Mayo festivals held throughout the Bay Area. Plan to spend the better part of a day.

Independence Day Fireworks and Celebrations
JULY 4

Anywhere in the Bay Area on July 4, your family is not far from an old-fashioned parade, celebration and fireworks display. Fireworks generally start around 9:30 pm, but most cities have fun activities for kids throughout the day. The following list provides a sample of some of the major events. There are plenty more—some perhaps in your own neighborhood.

San Francisco Marina
(adjacent to Marina Blvd.
from Crissey Field to Fort Mason),
San Francisco
(415) 777-7120

Sponsored by the *San Francisco Chronicle*, this is "The City" in full party mode. There is live entertainment, food, and arts and crafts throughout the day from Marina Green to Pier 39, with a spectacular fireworks show in the evening. For the urban family, this is the real thing. Others may want to avoid the crowds and fog and attend one of the following events.

Berkeley Marina
(at the foot of University Ave.), Berkeley
(510) 644-6639

The City of Berkeley sponsors a glorious fireworks display at the end of the pier. Parking in the Marina lots is limited and once space is filled, no traffic is allowed over the I-80 overpass. The roads however are open to pedestrians. If you have small children, it is best to get there early since the return journey on foot may exhaust young kids.

Jack London Square
(on The Embarcadero
at the foot of Broadway), Oakland
(510) 627-1670

Festivities begin at noon with live music on two stages. There is an All-American Apple Bake-Off Contest, an inflatable playground, a canine obstacle course with demonstrations and an annual Kids' Hat and Flag Parade. Fireworks, which are launched from the estuary, can be observed from the Marina area (though it does get crowded). Other nearby viewing areas are Laney College and Alameda.

Marin Civic Center
(Civic Center Dr.), San Rafael
(415) 499-6400

Fireworks are held in conjunction with the Marin County Fair. Admission is charged however it includes all rides. Adults $10, seniors and children under 13 $8.

Redwood City
(650) 780-7311

This all-day festival begins with a pancake breakfast followed by a parade. In the afternoon there is music, food, arts and crafts, a kids' play area and a classic car show. Fireworks take place over the Port of Redwood City.

Bay Meadows Race Track
2600 S. Delaware St., San Mateo
(650) 348-7600

The City of San Mateo sponsors a family day and a fireworks show.

Pillar Point Harbor
(650) 579-9271

Fireworks take place between Pacifica and Half Moon Bay. Earlier in the day there is a parade and festival in Half Moon Bay.

Good Spirits Soaring
BERKELEY KITE FESTIVAL

Cesar E. Chavez Park (Berkeley Marina), Berkeley
(510) 235-5483
www.HighlineKites.com

E ven the simplest kite is magic—the Berkeley Kite Festival manages to multiply that magic a thousandfold. Held aloft by the brisk winds of the Bay with the Golden Gate Bridge as a backdrop, this astounding event features the wild, the unusual and the colorful. Your kids will see hundred-foot-long giant dragons or squid kites, as well as all the standards; diamond, serpent and box kites. Kids of all ages will find themselves swept away by the trick flying and playful fighter competitions. They will soon want to try their own hands at getting a kite aloft. Kite-making demonstrations, food, a candy drop, Taiko drumming and live music round out the day.

SEASONS AND TIMES
➤ One weekend in July: 11 am—5 pm. Call for specific date.

COST
➤ Free.

GETTING THERE
➤ By car, from I-80 N. or S. in Berkeley, take the University Ave. Exit west and continue for a mile. The limited on-site parking is free. About 5 minutes from the freeway.
➤ By public transit, take AC Transit bus 51 to the marina.

COMMENT
➤ Bring jackets and plan to make a day of it.

Climb Aboard Matey
FESTIVAL OF THE SEA

Hyde St. Pier, San Francisco
(415) 561-6662
www.maritime.org

C elebrating San Francisco's fishing tradition, this annual weekend-long festival overflows with family entertainment. There is international maritime music, food, interactive living history demonstrations, boat rides, a boat-building contest and a tugboat rodeo. A designated activity area offers kids the chance to make their own miniature boats. They'll learn how to catch crabs right off the pier and enjoy an old salt story and puppet show.

SEASONS AND TIMES

➤ One weekend in early September, 10 am—6 pm. Call for specific dates.

COST

➤ Hyde St. Pier admission prices (historic fleet, tours, programs and exhibits): Adults $5, seniors (over 62) and juniors (12 to 17) $2, under 12 free with an adult.

GETTING THERE

➤ Street parking is limited around the north end of Hyde St. near the pier. Lot parking while available, is expensive.

➤ By public transit, take Muni buses 19, 30 or 42 to the pier. Or take the Powell-Hyde cable car.

COMMENT

➤ Include a visit to the submarine USS *Pampanito*, Fisherman's Wharf or any of the other sites along the Marina and plan to make a day of it.

Groovin' on a Sunday Afternoon
SOLANO STROLL

**Solano Ave. (between San Pablo Ave.
and The Alameda), Berkeley
(510) 527-5538
www.solanoavenuestroll.org**

Well beyond the biggest block party of your imagination, the Solano Stroll festivities extend the entire length of the Solano Avenue commercial district. For one day a year, the district is closed to traffic and turned into a giant pedestrian street fair.

The event begins with an astonishingly small-town-style parade that features marching bands, carnival dancers, fire engines, Scout packs and troops, local officials and a few collectible cars. Booths from local businesses and civic organizations, fair style events and entertainers line the streets. There is plenty of food from local restaurants, as well as rock bands, ethnic music and a bicycle ramp-jumping demonstration. A dunking tank is always a favorite with kids, who line up to throw a ball and drop a willing victim into the water.

SEASONS AND TIMES
➤ One Sunday in early September. Call for specific date.

COST
➤ Free.

GETTING THERE
➤ By car, from I-80 N. or S., take the Albany Exit or Buchanan St. Exit (the signs differ depending on which direction you are coming from). Follow the signs to Marin Ave. headed east until you cross San Pablo Ave. Park anywhere on Marin and walk 1 block north to Solano. About 5 minutes from the freeway.
➤ By public transit, take AC Transit buses 7, 15, 43 or 67.

Celebrating all
that is Berkeley
BERKELEY PARADE
AND FESTIVAL

**Civic Center Park, (ML King, Jr. Way between Center St.
and Allston Way), Berkeley
(510) 849-4688
www.howberkeleycanyoube.com**

T he city with a reputation for zaniness cele-
brates everything that has become a household
name in this entertaining parade and festival.
While many parades seem to be an opportunity for
commercial floats and advertising, this one embraces
every form of exhibitionism. Organizers seek out
funny, irreverent and provocative participants—from
men in grass suits and cars with giant green lips, to
pink guys on unicycles. In all, over 75 organizations
representing Berkeley's different cultural, political
and ethnic groups participate in the parade. It follows
University Avenue to Shattuck Avenue, turns right at
Center Street and ends at Civic Center Park. The
festival has an outdoor stage and offers a full day of
live music, dance and the political satire of the San
Francisco Mime Troupe. On-site booths sell food
and drink, and there are crafts, children's art
workshops and other activities.

SEASONS AND TIMES
➤ One Sunday in September. Call for specific date and times.

COST
➤ Free.

GETTING THERE
➤ By car, from I-80 N. or S. in Berkeley, take the University Ave. Exit and head east to ML King, Jr. Way. Parking is available at municipal and private lots in the downtown area. About 10 minutes from the freeway.
➤ By public transit, take BART to the Berkeley Downtown Station. Or take AC Transit buses 7, 8, 9, 15, 40, 43, 51, 64, 65, 67 or F.

COMMENT
➤ This is Berkeley. That means you will see colorful characters and occasionally some nudity or profanity. Plan a 3- to 4-hour visit.

Rev Up Your Engines for FLEET WEEK

From the Ferry Building to Marina Green, San Francisco
Call Pier 39 at (415) 705-5500
www.fleetweek.com

The last Navy vessel home-ported in San Francisco has long departed, but the nostalgia and glamour survive in Fleet Week celebrations. The highlight is the aerial acrobatics of the Blue Angels. Everyone enjoys the breathtaking performance of these Navy jets and their incredibly skilled pilots. For best viewing, find a spot on the edge of the Bay so you can see the planes sweep under the Gate. If you are at Marina Green, you can also partake in a fair.

The second element of this festival is the Parade of Ships that steams under the Golden Gate Bridge. This is the Navy's show and they do themselves proud. They send an impressive variety of vessels, including aircraft carriers, submarines, destroyers and Coast Guard cutters to name a few. Ships are moored at San Francisco, Oakland and Alameda piers and are open for public visits for several days. Group tours can be arranged by calling the Navy information line at (510) 263-1803.

SEASONS AND TIMES
➤ Most of the festivities take place over one weekend in October. The Navy vessels are usually open for tours throughout the week. Call for specific dates and times.

COST
➤ Free.

GETTING THERE
➤ Street parking in the area is limited and expensive. Use public transit if you can.
➤ By public transit, take Muni buses 19, 30 or 42. Or take the Muni Metro (Line F) to the end of the line at Jones St.

COMMENT
➤ Everybody becomes a kid when the Blue Angels perform, but for those with Navy blood it is paradise. Plan on visiting a few hours, more if you want to tour the ships.

Frightfully Delightful HALLOWEEN FESTIVALS

"Trick-or-treating" and Halloween parties are still very much a fixture of American life. Many families, especially those with young children, look for more structured, safer ways to celebrate. Here are a few of the public events that cater to young children.

The Cannery
2801 Leavenworth St., San Francisco
(415) 771-3112

Costume contest, arts and crafts, cookie decorating, entertainment and trick-or-treating in Cannery shops and restaurants.

Trick or Treat
Down 4th Street Parade, San Rafael
(415) 457-2266

Local merchants provide the treats, while parents and kids provide the gaiety.

Jack London Square
(on The Embarcadero at the foot of Broadway), Oakland
(510) 627-1670

Halloween at the Square runs from 10 am to 3 pm. It features a scavenger hunt, craft center and a free costume contest with awards given in several categories. There is a small fee for the carnival games and scarecrow stuffing.

Deck the Halls
CHRISTMAS TREE LIGHTING CEREMONIES AND FESTIVITIES

If you want snow, you will have to get in your car and drive east. If you're looking for the holiday spirit, lots of fun and the chance to stroll outdoors in our crisp Decembers, check out some of these special events that grace the season.

Pier 39
Ghiradelli Square and The Cannery, San Francisco
(415) 626-7070

Each of the major shopping complexes in the Fisherman's Wharf area features a tree lighting ceremony, Christmas festivities with entertainment, caroling and visits from Santa.

The Hyde St. Pier
San Francisco
(415) 561-666

The Maritime Museum offers children several seasonal programs with sea themes.

Jack London Square
(on The Embarcadero at the foot of Broadway),
Oakland
(510) 627-1670

Schoolchildren help decorate a 70-foot fir tree at this festival held on the day after Thanksgiving. There is live entertainment before and after the lighting, a gospel sing-along, craft booths, face painting and more.

San Rafael Parade of Lights/Winter Wonderland
(415) 457-2266

Surprise! There is snow after all. Tons of snow appears on Fourth Street in San Rafael, just in time for a visit from Santa, Mrs. Claus and the reindeer.

Room & Board

KID-FRIENDLY RESTAURANTS

E ating out with the family offers numerous rewards, chief among them that someone else does the cooking and dishes. Luckily, there is no shortage of restaurants in the Bay Area that provide a great experience for families. Each offers a fun atmosphere, good food that's reasonably priced and the staff is friendly. Most of the restaurants listed below offer kids' menus or kid-sized portions upon request, booster and high chairs, crayons and paper to keep little hands occupied. Many accommodate nursing moms, too, and provide baby changing stations.

Andale Taqueria
(Mexican served cafeteria-style)
2150 Chestnut St., San Francisco (415) 749-0506

Benihana
(Your at-table chef provides a show as well as a meal; expensive)
1737 Post St., San Francisco (415) 563-4844
1496 Old Bayshore Hwy., Burlingame (650) 342-5202

Bill's Place
(Kids' menu; old-fashioned burgers and shakes; crayons)
2315 Clement St., San Francisco (415) 221-5262)

Cactus Taqueria
(Cafeteria style service; large portions; tasty but not too spicy for kids)
1881 Solano Ave., Berkeley (510) 528-1881
5525 College Ave., Oakland (510) 547-1305

California Café
(Kids' menu; crayons, booster seats and highchairs available)
1736 Redwood Hwy., Corte Madera (415) 924-2233
700 Welch Rd., Palo Alto (650) 325-2233

California Pizza Kitchen
(Fun décor; large variety of pizzas)
438 Geary St., San Francisco (415) 563-8911

Chevys
(Tex-Mex; fun atmosphere, decent food, moderate prices; crayons; entertaining mechanical tortilla-maker)
150 Fourth St., San Francisco (415) 543-8060
3251 - 20th Ave., San Francisco (415) 665-8705
2 Embarcadero Ave., San Francisco (415) 391-2323
2400 Mariner Sq. Dr., Alameda (510) 521-3768
1890 Powell St., Emeryville (510) 768-1500
32 Bon Air Dr., Greenbrae (415) 461-3203

Fatapple's Restaurant and Bakery
(Hamburgers, pasta and great desserts; casual atmosphere)
7525 Fairmount Ave., El Cerrito (510) 528-3433
1346 Martin Luther King Jr. Way, Berkeley (510) 526-2260

Hard Rock Café
(Kids' menu; rock legends memorabilia; fun atmosphere)
1699 Van Ness Ave., San Francisco (415) 885-1699

Houlihan's Restaurant
(Potato skins; great views of the Bay and San Francisco)
600 Bridgeway, Sausalito (415) 332-8512

Long Life Noodle Company & Jook Joint
(Over 30 Asian noodle dishes)
139 Steuart St., San Francisco (415) 281-3818

Max's Diner
(Fun deli-atmosphere; friendly service; large portions)
311 Third St., San Francisco (415) 546-6297

Max's Opera Café
(Tasty food; singing staff floor show; huge desserts;
fun atmosphere)
601 Van Ness Ave., San Francisco (415) 771-7300
1250 Old Bayshore, Burlingame (415) 342-6297

Mel's Drive-In
(1950s-style diner; juke boxes, great burgers, fries
and shakes)
3355 Geary Blvd., San Francisco (415) 387-2255

Mo's Burgers
(Best burgers and milkshakes in town)
1322 Grant Ave., San Francisco (415) 788-3779

Planet Hollywood
(Star memorabilia; kids' menu; fun atmosphere,
gift shop)
2 Stockton St., San Francisco (415) 421-7827

Pasta Pomodoro
(Good food; inexpensive; Italian fare)
2027 Chestnut St., San Francisco (415) 474-3400
816 Irving St., San Francisco (415) 566-0900
2304 Market St., San Francisco (415) 558-8123
655 Union St., San Francisco (415) 788-3779

Tommaso's
(Pizza place; family oriented; fun atmosphere)
1042 Kearny St., San Francisco (415) 398-9696

World Wrapps
(Inexpensive; large portions; amazing selection)
2257 Chestnut St., San Francisco (415) 563-9727
2227 Polk St., San Francisco (415) 931-9727
1318 Burlingame Ave., Burlingame (415) 342-9777

Zachary's Chicago Pizza
(High-quality pizza; lively atmosphere)
1853 Solano Ave., Berkeley (510) 525-5950
5801 College Ave., Oakland (510) 655-6385

FAMILY-FRIENDLY HOTELS

L ooking for home-away-from-home comfort when you are on vacation? Face it, staying at a hotel can be hectic when you're traveling as a family. New surroundings, an unfamiliar bed—it can unsettle even the most adventurous child. Whether your stay in the Bay Area is a few days or a couple of weeks, the family-friendly establishments below will make sure your brood wakes up refreshed and ready to take on a new day. In addition to providing a comfortable atmosphere, some of these hotels offer family discounts, refrigerators and suites.

Value

Cow Hollow Motor Inn & Suites
(One and two bedroom suites; $10 extra per person)
2190 Lombard St., San Francisco (415) 921-5800

Best Western Flamingo Inn
(Under 18 stay free; family suites; free shuttle to Union Square; heated pool and sauna; restaurant; in-room movies and Nintendo™)
114 Seventh St., San Francisco (415) 621-0701

Moderate

Best Western Americania
(Under 18 stay free; family suites; free shuttle to Union Square; heated pool and sauna; restaurant; in-room movies and Nintendo™)
121 Seventh St., San Francisco (415) 626-0200

Best Western Carriage Inn
(Under 18 stay free; family suites; free shuttle to Union Square; heated pool and sauna; restaurant; in-room movies and Nintendo™)
140 Seventh St., San Francisco (415) 552-8600

The Monarch Hotel
(Under 18 stay free; cable television; game room)
1015 Geary St., San Francisco (415) 673-5232

Redwood Inn
(Under 5 stay free; some rooms with kitchenettes; cribs and rollaway beds extra)
1530 Lombard St., San Francisco (415) 776-3800

Stanyan Park Hotel
(One and two bedroom suites; continental breakfast included, free cribs; rollaway beds extra)
750 Stanyan St., San Francisco (415) 751-1000

The Wharf Inn
(Up to four people in room for same price; free parking; babysitting services available)
2601 Mason St., San Francisco (415) 673-7411

Expensive

Radisson Hotel at the Wharf
(Under 18 stay free; cribs free; refrigerators and Nintendo™ in room)
250 Beach St., San Francisco (415) 392-6700

Sheraton at Fisherman's Wharf
(Cribs free; Nintendo™ in room; babysitting services
available; pool and gym; rollaway beds extra)
2500 Mason St., San Francisco (415) 362-5500

12 Months of Fun
DIRECTORY OF EVENTS

JANUARY
January through April
Whales, Wildlife & Wildflowers
Bear Valley Visitor Center, Pt.
Reyes National Seashore
(415) 499-5000
www.nps.gov/ggnra

Late January
Gold Discovery Day
Marshall Gold Discovery State
Historic Park, Coloma
(530) 622-3470
http://coloma.com

FEBRUARY
Early February through late March
Napa Valley Mustard Festival
Various Napa Valley locations
(707) 259-9020
www.mustardfestival.org

Mid-February to early March
Fat Tuesday
Cannery Row, Monterey
(831) 658-5205
www.bluefinbilliards.com

Mid-February to mid-March
Chinese New Year
Various locations around San
Francisco
(415) 982-3000
www.c-c-c.org/

Late February through early March
Snowfest Winter Carnival
North Lake Tahoe
(775) 832-7625
www.snowfest.com

MARCH
Early March
San Francisco Celtic Music and
Arts Festival
Fort Mason
(415) 252-9992
www.iaf.org/Festival.html

Mid-March
Tall Ships Tour
Fisherman's Wharf
(800) 200-5239

March to June (one weekend, date varies annually)
Mariposa Living History Days
History Center and downtown,
Mariposa
(209) 966-3685

APRIL
Early April
Street Performers Festival
Pier 39
(415) 705-5500
www.pier39.com

Early to mid-April
Fisherman's Festival
West Side Park, Bodega Bay
(707) 875-3704
www.bodegabay.org

Mid-April
San Jose Children's Faire
Children's Discovery Museum,
San Jose
(408) 277-2617

Mid to late April
Cherry Blossom Festival
Japantown
(415) 563-2313

Mid to late April
Apple Blossom Festival
Main Street, Sebastopol
(877) 828-4748
www. sebastopol.org

Mid-April to mid-May
Carnaval
Various locations around San
Francisco
(415) 826-1401
www.meca.bigstep.com

Late April
Native American Strawberry
Celebration
Kule Loklo, Pt. Reyes National
Seashore
(415) 464-5100
www.nps.gov/pore

Late April
Cal Day
University of California, Berkeley
(510) 642-5215
www.berkeley.edu/calday

Late April
Pacific Coast Dream Machines
Show
Half Moon Bay Airport, Half
Moon Bay
(650) 726-2328

Late April
Butter & Egg Days Parade
Historic Downtown, Petaluma
(707) 778-3491
www.butterandeggdays.com

MAY
Weekend closest to May 5
Cinco de Mayo
Various locations around San
Francisco
(415) 826-1401
www.meca.bigstep.com

Early to Mid-May
San Francisco Youth Arts Festival
Zeum
(415) 759-2916
www.youth-arts.com

Mid-May
Civil War Land & Sea Battle
Angel Island
(415) 435-5390
www.cal-parks.ca.gov

JUNE
Early June
Union Street Arts Festival
Cow Hollow District
(510) 970-3217

Early to mid-June
Fiesta Filipina
San Francisco Civic Center Plaza
(650) 757-4803

**Early June to late August
(Sundays)**
Stern Grove Midsummer Music
Festival
Stern Grove
(415) 252-6253

Mid-June
North Beach Festival
Grant Avenue and Green Street
(415) 989-2220

Mid-June
Juneteenth Celebration
Kimball Park
(415) 229-1220

JULY
Mid-July
Cable Car Bell-Ringing
Competition
Union Square
(415) 923-6217
www.sfcablecar.com

Late July
Berkeley Kite Festival
Berkeley Marina
(510) 235-5483
www.HighlineKites.com

AUGUST
Early August
Nihonmachi Street Fair
Japantown and Japan Center
(415) 771-9861

Early August
Multi-Cultural Kite Festival
Golden Gate Park
(415) 750-5110
www.frp.org/kitefestival.html

SEPTEMBER
Early September
Festival of the Sea
Hyde Street Pier
(415) 561-6662
www.maritime.org

Early September
Ghirardelli Square Chocolate
Festival
Ghirardelli Square
(415) 775-5500
www.GhirardelliSq.com

Early September
Solano Stroll
Solano Ave., Berkeley
(510) 527-5538
www.solanoavenuestroll.org

Early September
Sausalito Art Festival
Marinship Park, Sausalito
(415) 332-3555

Mid-September
Latino Summer Fiesta
Civic Center Plaza
(415) 826-1401

Mid-September
Italian Festa
Jack London Square, Oakland
(510) 814-6000

Late September
How Berkeley Can You Be?
Downtown and Martin Luther
King Park, Berkeley
(510) 849-4688
www.howberkeleycanyoube.com

**Late September to late
October**
Jazz at Ghirardelli
Ghirardelli Square
(415) 775-5500
www.GhirardelliSq.com

OCTOBER
Early October
Fleet Week
Various locations on waterfront
(415) 705-5500
www.fleetweek.com

Mid-October
Italian Heritage Parade and
Festival (Columbus Day Parade)
North Beach and Fisherman's
Wharf
(415) 989-2220

Late October
Great Halloween & Pumpkin
Festival
West Portal
(415) 249-4625

Late October
Half Moon Bay Art & Pumpkin
Festival
Main Street, Half Moon Bay
(650) 726-9652

NOVEMBER
Mid-November
Harvest Festival and Christmas
Crafts Market
Concourse Exhibition Center
(707) 778-6300

DECEMBER
Early December
Christmas at Sea
Hyde Street Pier
(415) 561-6662
www.maritime.org

INDEX